A PURPOSE DRIVEN

FEDERAL RETIREMENT

A

PURPOSE DRIVEN FEDERAL RETIREMENT

How to Turn Your Federal Employee Benefits Into the Life You've Been Planning For

STUART HUNSICKER

Founder, Purpose Driven Retirement Planners

PURPOSE DRIVEN PRESS

Richmond, Virginia

A Purpose Driven Federal Retirement

How to Turn Your Federal Employee Benefits Into the Life You've Been Planning For

This book provides general educational information and is not individualized financial, investment, tax, legal, accounting, insurance, federal-benefits, estate-planning, or medical advice. Laws, rules, thresholds, agency procedures, plan features, and carrier arrangements change. Verify current information with the responsible agency and qualified professionals before acting. The author and publisher are not affiliated with or endorsed by the United States government or any federal agency.

Detailed disclosures and selected primary references appear at the back of the book.

Published by Purpose Driven Press

Richmond, Virginia

ISBN: 979-8-9977452-7-1

First edition, 2026

PDRPlanners.com

Dedication

To my wife, Andrea, and our children—

for the love, patience, laughter, and purpose you bring to my life.

To my family and my faith, which continually remind me that success is measured by more than what we accumulate.

To the team at Purpose Driven Retirement Planners—

thank you for helping turn good intentions into meaningful action.

And to the clients I have had the privilege to serve over the years—

your questions, experiences, challenges, and dreams helped shape

the perspective I now bring to the people we serve.

Contents

Contents, continued

A Note to the Reader

This Is a Guide, Not a One-Time Read

You do not need to memorize this book. That would be a poor use of retirement—and possibly a violation of several personal promises involving golf, travel, grandchildren, or sleeping past 6:00 a.m.

Use it as a guide. Mark it up. Write in the margins. Complete the questions and action steps. Return to the relevant chapters when retirement approaches, when benefits begin, when Medicare or Social Security enters the picture, when tax laws change, when a spouse dies, when health changes, or when the life you want begins to look different.

Federal retirement is not one decision. It is a sequence of decisions. Your pension, TSP, Social Security, FEHB or PSHB, Medicare, taxes, insurance, survivor protection, estate plan, long-term-care strategy, and life goals must continue working together as circumstances change.

The Question Behind Every Chapter

What matters most to you?

That question is not decoration. It is the standard against which every benefit and strategy should be measured. A decision is not successful merely because it follows a rule or produces an attractive number. It should move you closer to the people, experiences, security, generosity, independence, and purpose you said mattered.

How to Use This Book

Each time you return to a chapter, move through the same five-part rhythm:

Purpose. Identify what the decision is meant to accomplish.

Benefits and strategy. Understand the federal rules, resources, and planning choices involved.

Risks. Ask what could interfere with the outcome—and who else could be affected.

Action. Choose the next concrete step, person, document, or deadline.

Review. Revisit the decision when laws, benefits, markets, health, family, or purpose changes.

Information Is Not the Finish Line

A doctor can explain the test results, the risks, and the treatment. The information becomes valuable only when the patient acts. Retirement planning works the same way.

Reading about an incorrect service record does not correct it. Understanding survivor benefits does not protect a spouse until the election and surrounding plan are addressed. Knowing that pretax money may create future RMD and IRMAA problems does not create a tax strategy. Awareness is the diagnosis. Action is the treatment.

Use this guide to learn, verify, decide, and act. Then return when life gives you a new reason to ask the question again: What matters most now?

Introduction

Your Federal Benefits Are Valuable—But They Are Not a Retirement Plan

Federal employees often spend an entire career building one of the most valuable collections of retirement benefits available to American workers.

There may be a pension through the Federal Employees Retirement System. There is usually a Thrift Savings Plan account, potentially containing both traditional and Roth money. Social Security may provide another source of lifetime income. Federal Employees Health Benefits coverage may continue into retirement. Federal Employees' Group Life Insurance may remain in force in some form. Depending on the employee's position and history, there may also be military-service credit, special retirement provisions, unused sick-leave credit, a FERS retirement supplement, or survivor benefits for a spouse.

On paper, that can look like a retirement plan.

But it isn't one.

It is a collection of benefits. A retirement plan is what turns those benefits into a coordinated strategy for the life you actually want to live.

That distinction is the reason for this book.

Benefit Rich, but Decision Heavy

Federal employment offers real advantages. It also creates an unusually complicated retirement decision.

A private-sector employee may primarily need to decide when to stop working, when to claim Social Security, and how to use a 401(k). A federal employee can face all of those questions while also deciding when an annuity should begin, whether a retirement is immediate, postponed, or deferred, whether a survivor benefit should be elected, whether health and life insurance can continue, how TSP withdrawals should be structured, and how every choice affects a spouse.

Those decisions do not live in separate boxes.

The survivor election can affect the pension check, but it can also affect whether an eligible surviving spouse may continue FEHB coverage. The date you separate can influence retirement eligibility and access to retirement funds. The decision to postpone an annuity can reduce or avoid an age-based pension reduction, yet it may temporarily suspend health and life insurance coverage. A large traditional TSP balance can provide flexibility, but withdrawals may increase taxable income, make more Social Security taxable, or trigger higher Medicare premiums through IRMAA.

A decision that looks attractive when viewed by itself can become expensive when viewed as part of the entire household.

That is why federal retirement planning requires more than collecting benefit estimates. It requires coordination.

Retirement Eligibility Is Not Retirement Readiness

Many federal employees understandably organize retirement around a date.

They know their Minimum Retirement Age. They count their years of service. They watch the calendar for the moment they reach an age-and-service combination that allows them to leave. Some have even kept a running countdown for years.

Reaching that date can be exciting. But eligibility answers only one question:

Am I permitted to retire under the rules?

It does not necessarily answer the more important questions:

Will my income support the life I want? What will arrive in my bank account after taxes, insurance premiums, and survivor reductions? How will I cover expenses while my claim is being processed? Should Social Security begin immediately or later? How much can I safely withdraw from TSP? What happens to my spouse if I die first? Will our healthcare strategy still work after Medicare begins? What happens if inflation, a bear market, or a long-term-care need changes the plan?

A person can be fully eligible to retire and still be financially or emotionally unprepared for retirement. The opposite can also be true: someone may have sufficient resources but continue working because the federal benefit system feels too complicated to leave behind confidently.

The goal is not simply to identify the first day you are allowed to retire. The goal is to find the point when your benefits, finances, family protections, and vision for life come together.

Your Human Resources Office Has an Important—but Limited—Role

Federal human resources professionals perform essential work. They help employees understand eligibility, process forms, assemble records, and move retirement applications through the system. But an HR office generally cannot build a comprehensive financial plan for your household.

It may explain what survivor elections are available. It is not necessarily responsible for determining whether a particular election, combined with your spouse's income, life insurance, Social Security, healthcare needs, and other assets, is appropriate for your family.

It may provide an annuity estimate. It may not calculate how the estimate interacts with federal and state taxes, Medicare premiums, TSP withdrawals, inflation, or the loss of one Social Security benefit after the first spouse dies.

It may tell you that you can retire. It cannot decide what you are retiring to.

That is not a criticism of HR. It is a recognition that benefit administration and retirement planning are different jobs. You need accurate information from your agency and the government programs administering your benefits. You also need a process that connects those facts to your actual life.

Why Specialized Federal-Benefits Training Matters

Federal benefits have their own terminology, calculations, elections, deadlines, and exceptions. A financial professional can be experienced with investments and still have limited familiarity with the rules affecting federal employees.

The Chartered Federal Employee Benefits Consultant℠, or ChFEBC℠, designation represents specialized training for financial professionals in federal employee benefits and the planning issues surrounding them. My work as a ChFEBC℠ and Federal Retirement Consultant℠ (FRC℠) has reinforced a lesson that will appear throughout this book: the value of a federal benefit is determined not only by what it pays, but by how well it is coordinated with everything else.

A designation does not replace the need to verify current law, agency records, plan documents, or an individual employee's circumstances. It also does not guarantee a particular result. It does, however, help identify a financial professional who has invested time in understanding a benefit system that operates differently from most private-sector retirement programs.

Federal employees should not feel embarrassed if the system seems confusing. It is confusing. The answer is not to memorize every regulation. It is to understand the decisions that matter, know what information must be verified, and recognize how one election can affect the rest of the plan.

The Pension Is Not the Purpose

It is easy for retirement planning to become a conversation about formulas.

We calculate a high-3 average salary. We count years and months of creditable service. We review TSP balances and Social Security estimates. We compare survivor reductions. We estimate taxes and healthcare premiums.

All of that work matters. But none of those numbers tells us why you want to retire.

Do you want more time with your spouse? Do you want to travel while you are healthy enough to enjoy it? Are you hoping to help with grandchildren, care for an aging parent, serve in your church, start a second career, volunteer, relocate, or simply regain control of your days? Do you want to leave a financial legacy, or would you rather use more of your resources while you are alive to create experiences with the people you love?

Your benefits are not the destination. They are tools.

The pension can help provide dependable income. TSP can provide flexibility and growth. Social Security can create inflation-adjusted lifetime income. FEHB can help protect access to healthcare. Survivor benefits and life insurance can help protect the people who depend on you.

But the purpose of those benefits is not to produce the largest possible statement. Their purpose is to support a life.

The question is not merely, "What are my federal benefits worth?"
The better question is, "What do I need my federal benefits to do?"

The Federal Retirement Paycheck

For most of your career, your financial life has been organized around a paycheck. Money arrives on a predictable schedule. Retirement contributions, taxes, insurance premiums, and other deductions occur before the balance reaches your bank account.

Retirement changes that system.

Your FERS or CSRS annuity may arrive from one source. Social Security may arrive from another. TSP withdrawals may need to be created intentionally. A spouse may have a separate pension, retirement account, or Social Security benefit. Taxes may no longer be withheld in the same manner. Some payroll deductions disappear, while healthcare, life insurance, Medicare, or other costs remain.

The pieces may be valuable, but someone still has to assemble them into a paycheck.

That paycheck should do more than cover this month's bills. It should be resilient enough to withstand changing markets, inflation, tax-law changes, healthcare costs, and the death of either spouse. It should allow you to enjoy retirement without making every purchase feel like a threat to your future.

A successful federal retirement is not created by maximizing every benefit independently. It is created by coordinating the benefits around the household's priorities.

The Doctor Story: Information Is Not Treatment

There is another reason federal employees need a clear process: knowing what to do and completing it are not the same thing.

Imagine going to your doctor for a routine physical.

During the appointment, you mention how excited you are that your daughter is getting married. You talk about becoming a grandparent someday and all the things you hope to do with your family.

A few days later, the doctor calls with the test results. Your cholesterol is dangerously high. Your blood pressure is much higher than it should be. Changes need to be made. Maybe that means medication. Maybe it means changing your diet, exercising more, or finally admitting that a doughnut is not a breakfast vegetable.

Then the doctor connects the diagnosis to what matters most: if you do not make some changes, you may not be healthy enough—or even be around—to enjoy the family milestones you just described.

Imagine responding, "Thanks for letting me know. Let me think about it."

Put that way, the response sounds strange. Yet people do something similar with financial planning all the time.

The physical was the planning process. The test results were the analysis. But the diagnosis alone does not lower blood pressure or cholesterol. The prescription only helps when the patient fills it, takes it, and follows through. Financial planning works the same way: the recommendations are not the result. Implementation is the treatment.

They identify the people and experiences that matter most. They review their federal benefits. They discover a gap in survivor income, an outdated beneficiary, an approaching FEHB deadline, a tax problem inside TSP, or a retirement date that does not work quite the way they assumed. They learn what could improve the plan—and then they wait.

Sometimes they wait for months. Sometimes they wait for years. Sometimes the federal government changes three forms and a website while they are thinking about it, just to keep things interesting.

The problem is not that people do not care. Change is difficult. Retirement decisions involve paperwork, taxes, investments, insurance choices, permanent elections, uncertainty, and emotion. Doing nothing can feel safer.

But doing nothing is still a decision. And sometimes inaction is one of the greatest risks to a federal retirement plan.

Information can reveal the path, but information cannot walk it for you. If the retirement vision you described is something you truly want to achieve, the necessary decisions must eventually become completed actions. A retirement estimate left in a folder cannot protect a spouse. An unsigned beneficiary form cannot direct a benefit. A good intention cannot repair a service record after a deadline has passed.

Retirement applications require documentation. Military-service deposits must be addressed at the appropriate time. Personnel records may need to be corrected. Beneficiary designations can become outdated after marriage, divorce, death, or the birth of a child. Survivor choices are made on retirement forms that may feel administrative even though they can shape a family's financial security for decades.

People often delay because the decision feels permanent, the paperwork feels intimidating, or the number of moving parts makes it easier to keep working one more year.

A good plan should reduce that friction. It should identify the decisions, place them in the right order, assign deadlines, and make clear which information still needs to be confirmed. Planning tells you what matters. Implementation helps make sure it happens.

How to Use This Book

This book is designed to be used, not simply read.

We will begin with the life you want to create. Then we will organize your federal service history and benefits, examine the decisions that can change those benefits, and build a coordinated retirement-income strategy. We will address taxes, Social Security, TSP, FEHB, Medicare, FEGLI, survivor planning, long-term care, estate planning, and the transition out of federal service. Finally, we will return to health, relationships, contribution, legacy, and purpose—the things that make the financial work worthwhile.

Throughout the book, you will encounter Federal Benefits in Plain English, Common Federal Employee Mistakes, planning examples, questions to verify, and Purpose Driven Federal Employee Action Steps. These features are intended to help you turn information into decisions and decisions into action.

Read it from beginning to end the first time, but do not expect to be finished with it when you reach the last page. Federal retirement is not a single decision made on the day you submit an application. It is a series of decisions that continues through the final years of employment, the transition into retirement, the beginning of Social Security and Medicare, changing tax laws, market cycles, health events, family changes, and eventually survivor and legacy planning.

Return to the relevant chapters when life changes. Revisit the TSP discussion before changing an investment or withdrawal strategy. Review the survivor chapter before completing the retirement application. Return to the healthcare chapters before Medicare eligibility or an Open Season decision. Revisit the tax chapter before taking a large distribution or completing a Roth conversion. Come back to the purpose chapters when retirement begins to feel busy but not especially meaningful.

Think of this book less like a novel and more like a trusted field guide. Nobody reads a field guide once and then says, “Excellent. I now remember every trail, weather pattern, and mildly judgmental bear.” You keep it nearby because the information becomes useful at different points in the journey.

Write in the margins. Circle questions. Add dates. Use the action steps. Bring the book to conversations with your spouse, agency benefits office, tax professional, estate-planning attorney, insurance professional, or financial adviser. A useful retirement book should become more marked up as retirement gets closer.

Federal laws, regulations, plan provisions, administrative procedures, and benefit amounts change. Your employment history and family circumstances are also unique. Treat the examples as educational illustrations. Before acting, verify current rules with the appropriate agency, plan administrator, tax professional, attorney, insurance professional, or other qualified adviser.

You do not need to become an expert in every federal regulation. You do need to understand what is at stake, which questions to ask, and how the pieces of your retirement fit together.

Start With What Matters Most

Before we calculate a pension or discuss a TSP withdrawal, begin with a more personal question:

What matters most to you?

Your answer may be family, security, freedom, travel, health, service, faith, generosity, or simply the confidence that you will not become a burden to the people you love.

Write it down.

That answer will become the standard against which the decisions in this book are measured. A retirement choice is not automatically good because it produces the largest immediate check. It is good when it helps your household live the retirement you said you wanted while protecting the people and priorities that matter most.

You spent a career earning these benefits.

Now it is time to turn them into a life.

Your Purpose Driven Federal Employee Action Step

Before moving to Chapter 1, answer these questions in writing:

1. What are the three things I most want retirement to make possible?
2. Who besides me will be affected by my federal retirement decisions?
3. Which benefit or retirement decision currently creates the most uncertainty?
4. If I could replace uncertainty with confidence in one area, what would it be?
5. Am I planning only for the day I retire—or for the decades that may follow?

Do not worry about having perfect answers. The purpose is to establish the life your benefits will be asked to support. Every calculation that follows should connect back to that purpose.

Chapter 1

Retirement Isn't a Service Date

Federal employees are trained to think in dates.

There is a service computation date, a leave service computation date, a retirement service computation date, a date of career appointment, a date of birth, a Minimum Retirement Age, and—if you have ever tried to reconcile all of them—a date when you begin to wonder whether the government owns stock in calendars.

Dates matter. One day can affect eligibility, the beginning of an annuity, a leave payout, insurance continuation, or access to retirement money. Later in this book, we will treat those dates with the respect they deserve.

But a date cannot tell you whether you are ready to retire.

It cannot tell you what Tuesday morning will feel like after the retirement ceremony is over. It cannot tell you whether your spouse shares your vision, whether your income supports that vision, or whether leaving federal service will give you freedom or simply remove the structure that organized your life for decades.

Retirement eligibility is a rule. Retirement readiness is a life decision.

The Countdown Problem

Many federal employees begin counting down long before retirement. They know the month when they reach their MRA. They know when their twentieth, thirtieth, or thirty-fifth year of service arrives. Some can tell you the exact number of workdays remaining after subtracting weekends, holidays, annual leave, and the three meetings they have already decided not to attend.

There is nothing wrong with looking forward to retirement. A demanding career, a long commute, organizational changes, staffing shortages, or work that no longer feels meaningful can make the finish line especially attractive.

The danger is allowing the countdown to become the plan.

A countdown answers when you hope to leave. It does not answer what you are moving toward. If the only retirement objective is to stop working, success arrives on the first morning. Then what?

The better goal is not escape. It is transition—from a life organized by employment to a life organized by purpose.

Can Retire and Should Retire Are Different Questions

Federal retirement rules create eligibility combinations based on age, service, retirement coverage, and sometimes the employee's position or the circumstances of separation. Meeting one of those combinations may make an annuity available. It does not automatically make that retirement date financially wise.

Suppose an employee learns that retirement is technically available. The pension estimate looks reasonable, and the TSP balance is larger than it has ever been. The employee may understandably conclude, "I can retire."

But the estimate may be gross rather than spendable income. It may not reflect the survivor election, federal and state taxes, FEHB premiums, FEGLI costs, or other deductions.

The employee may be planning to claim Social Security later but have no clear income bridge. The spouse may expect to travel extensively while the employee expects to work part-time. One person may see the TSP as retirement income while the other sees it as untouchable long-term-care and legacy money.

Every assumption can be individually reasonable and collectively incompatible.

Eligibility is an important milestone. Readiness means the household understands how the pieces fit, what the tradeoffs are, and what life the benefits are expected to support.

The Golden Handcuffs Can Be Real

Federal benefits can make leaving emotionally difficult even when the numbers work.

An employee may worry about giving up a reliable paycheck, unused leave accrual, employer TSP contributions, FEHB coverage as an active employee, or the possibility of a larger pension after one more year. The phrase one more year can become a renewable subscription.

Sometimes another year is exactly the right decision. It may improve the high-3 average salary, add creditable service, reach a more favorable eligibility threshold, strengthen savings, or complete an insurance requirement. Working longer can also be the right personal choice when the work remains meaningful.

But another year should purchase something identifiable.

If working twelve more months produces a measurable improvement that matters to the plan, that is a strategy. If the employee continues working because nobody has converted the benefits into a clear retirement paycheck, that is uncertainty wearing a government badge.

Ask: What specifically does another year improve? How much does it improve it? What am I giving up in exchange?

Time has value too. A larger pension is valuable, but so is a healthy year with a spouse, an aging parent, children, grandchildren, friends, or a body still willing to get on an airplane without filing a complaint with management.

What Are You Retiring To?

The most useful retirement question is often not "When can I leave?" It is "What am I retiring to?"

That question can feel uncomfortable because work has answered so many other questions for so long. Work determines when you wake up, where you go, what problems need attention, who you interact with, and when you are allowed to take a vacation. It provides structure, identity, relationships, and a sense of usefulness—even on the days when it also provides six emails marked urgent that were clearly not urgent.

Retirement removes much of that structure at once.

Some people thrive immediately. Others discover that freedom is wonderful but surprisingly demanding. When every day is open, someone still has to decide what makes the day worthwhile.

A purpose driven federal retirement begins by identifying the people, experiences, responsibilities, and contributions that should fill the space previously occupied by work.

The Saturday Problem

Imagine the first Saturday after retirement. It may feel wonderful. There is no alarm, no commute, and no reason to look at the agency phone.

Now imagine the fiftieth Saturday.

Golf, gardening, travel, home projects, and time with family can create a rich retirement. But leisure alone may not provide enough purpose for every person. A forty-year career cannot always be replaced by a television remote and a very committed relationship with the hardware store.

This does not mean retirement needs another full-time job. It means sustainable retirement usually contains several ingredients: rest, relationships, health, learning, contribution, enjoyment, and something that makes the retiree feel useful.

The mix will differ. One person may consult ten hours a week. Another may volunteer, serve at church, help with grandchildren, coach, teach, travel, create art, care for family, or finally become the person who knows what every plant in the yard is called.

The goal is not to stay busy. Busyness can follow you into retirement without adding meaning. The goal is to use time intentionally.

The Three Stages of Federal Retirement

Retirement is rarely one unchanging period. It is more useful to think in stages.

The active years are often the years people picture first. Travel, hobbies, family experiences, home projects, and new adventures may be at their highest. Spending may be higher than expected because retirement finally creates the time to do the things that were postponed during a career.

The transitional years often bring a slower pace. Travel may become less frequent, priorities may shift closer to home, and routines become more established. Some expenses decline while healthcare and support costs begin to receive more attention.

The support years are when maintaining independence may become the central objective. Housing, transportation, healthcare, long-term care, family assistance, and financial simplicity matter more.

These stages do not begin at fixed ages. Health, family, and circumstance determine the timing. A useful plan prepares for all three without assuming the active years last forever—or acting as though they should not be enjoyed because the support years might eventually arrive.

Your Federal Benefits Need Jobs

Once the retirement vision becomes clearer, each federal benefit can be assigned a job.

The pension may cover a portion of essential monthly expenses. Social Security may provide inflation-adjusted lifetime income. TSP may fund the remaining paycheck, travel, emergencies, future care, or legacy goals. FEHB may protect access to healthcare. Survivor benefits and life insurance may protect a spouse. Cash reserves may bridge the period while the retirement claim is processed.

A benefit without a job is simply a number on a statement.

This is particularly important for TSP. Some employees say they do not intend to use it. They want to preserve it for long-term care or leave it to children. The intention is admirable, but the account still needs a tax strategy. Required distributions, Medicare IRMAA, survivor tax brackets, and inherited-account rules may eventually give the money a job the employee never chose.

We will address that problem in detail later. For now, remember this: not spending an account is not the same as planning it.

Define Enough Before the Government Defines It for You

Federal employees often ask whether they have enough to retire. Enough is not a universal number.

It depends on the income the household needs, the life it wants, the risks it must absorb, the legacy it hopes to create, and how much flexibility provides peace of mind. Two employees with identical pensions and TSP balances may need completely different plans.

One may have a paid-off home, modest spending, and a spouse with a pension. Another may support family members, carry a mortgage, travel extensively, or face significant healthcare concerns. Comparing balances without comparing lives is financial planning by photocopier.

Before deciding whether the numbers are enough, define what enough needs to accomplish.

A Purpose Driven Federal Retirement

A purpose driven retirement does not require a dramatic second act. It does not require starting a charity, climbing a mountain, or learning to make sourdough bread unless you genuinely want to do those things.

It requires alignment.

Your time, money, benefits, health, relationships, and decisions should increasingly support what matters most. That may mean adventure. It may mean service. It may mean family, faith, generosity, security, or the quiet freedom to control your own calendar.

The federal benefit system provides valuable tools. This book will help you understand them. But the rules cannot define a meaningful retirement for you.

That part is your decision.

Your Purpose Driven Federal Employee Action Step

Before calculating benefits, create a one-page retirement vision. Answer these questions:

1. If work no longer organized my days, what would I want a typical week to contain?

2. Which people and relationships do I want retirement to give me more time for?

3. What experiences do I want during the active years while my health and energy are strongest?

4. What would make me feel useful, connected, or purposeful after federal service?

5. What financial promises have I made—to a spouse, children, grandchildren, charities, or myself?

6. What am I afraid retirement could take away?

7. If I work one more year, what specific improvement am I purchasing—and what year of retirement am I giving up?

Then complete this sentence:

My federal benefits need to help me

________________________________.

Keep that sentence nearby. Every pension, TSP, Social Security, insurance, tax, and survivor decision in the chapters ahead should be evaluated against it.

Chapter 2

Where Are You Today?

Every useful map has a small dot that says, "You Are Here." It is not the most exciting part of the map, but without it the rest is decorative artwork.

Retirement planning works the same way. Before deciding when to retire, how to use the TSP, or whether the pension will be enough, you need an accurate picture of where you are today. That means gathering records, identifying assumptions, and discovering which facts still need to be verified.

This chapter may not produce the same emotional rush as imagining a month in Tuscany. It can, however, keep the Tuscany budget from being built on the wrong service date.

Financial Organization Is Financial Planning

People sometimes treat organization as clerical work that happens before financial planning begins. In reality, organization is part of the planning.

A pension estimate based on incomplete service history is not a plan. A TSP balance without knowing how much is traditional and how much is Roth is not a plan. A beneficiary intention that exists only in your head is not a beneficiary designation.

The objective is not to build a museum-quality filing cabinet. It is to create one reliable retirement record that you and your spouse or trusted person can understand. Paper, encrypted digital storage, or a combination can work. The system matters less than knowing where the information is and keeping it current.

Federal retirement planning is full of documents created at different times by different systems. Your job is to make those systems tell one coherent story.

Start With Your Federal Service Record

Begin with your Official Personnel Folder or electronic Official Personnel Folder and your history of personnel actions. OPM recommends reviewing the record years before retirement, not during the final week while somebody is also collecting signatures for your luncheon card.

Confirm the beginning and ending dates of every period of civilian service. Note transfers, breaks in service, part-time schedules, intermittent service, temporary appointments, changes in retirement coverage, promotions, and pay changes that may affect the high-3 average salary.

Collect the SF-50s that document the important events. The SF-50, Notification of Personnel Action, is evidence of what the agency recorded. It is valuable. It is not sacred scripture, and one SF-50 rarely tells your entire retirement story.

If something is missing or inconsistent, begin correcting it while you are still employed. Former employees can request records through the National Archives or the appropriate personnel records process, but solving a problem is generally easier while your agency personnel office and payroll history are still close at hand.

One Acronym, Several Dates

Federal employees quickly learn the initials SCD—Service Computation Date. The trouble is that the government uses service computation dates for different purposes. Naturally, it gave them similar names. Clarity would have made the forms too relaxing.

The SCD shown in Block 31 of the SF-50 is generally the service computation date used for leave accrual. It is not necessarily the date used to calculate retirement eligibility or the length of service in a pension computation.

Leave, retirement, reduction-in-force, and other benefit rules may credit service differently. Military service, refunded retirement deductions, temporary service, and breaks in service can affect the dates in different ways.

Do not copy the date from Block 31 into a retirement calculator and assume the case is closed. Ask for a retirement service history or estimate that identifies each period of service and shows how it is being treated. If two dates differ, do not merely choose the one you like better. Find out why.

Deposits, Redeposits, and Service That Needs Attention

Some periods of service may require a deposit or redeposit before they receive the retirement treatment you expect. The rules depend on the type and timing of the service, the retirement system, and whether deductions were taken or later refunded.

Examples can include nondeduction civilian service, service for which retirement contributions were refunded, or a period under a different appointment or retirement system.

Part-time and intermittent service can also affect eligibility and computation differently.

This is not an area for confident guessing. Obtain a written service history, identify any deposit or redeposit issue, request the cost and benefit impact, and evaluate the decision before retirement. "I thought that year counted" is a sentence best spoken during planning, not after the final pension has been adjudicated.

Military Service: Honorable Does Not Always Mean Creditable

Military service can be one of the most valuable—and most misunderstood—parts of a federal retirement record.

Eligible post-1956 military service may require a military service deposit to receive credit under the civilian retirement system. OPM generally advises that the deposit be completed before separation from federal employment. The exact rules can depend on retirement coverage, the dates and type of service, and whether military retired pay is involved.

A military service deposit may improve retirement eligibility, the pension computation, or both. But military time appearing in a leave service date does not prove it has been credited for retirement. Those are separate questions.

Gather the DD-214 or other discharge documentation, military earnings information, deposit calculation, payment records, and agency confirmation that the deposit is complete. If you made payments through payroll, preserve the final proof. Retirement planning should not rely on a faded memory that somebody in payroll said, "You should be all set."

Inventory the Income You Already Own

Next, list every potential source of retirement income and when it may begin.

For a FERS employee, that may include the basic annuity, the FERS annuity supplement if eligible, Social Security, TSP withdrawals, and income from a spouse's benefits or employment. A CSRS or CSRS Offset employee may have a different relationship among the civil service annuity, Social Security, and outside employment. Special-category employees may have distinct eligibility and computation rules.

Use current estimates, but label them as estimates. Record whether the pension amount is before or after a survivor election. Note whether taxes, FEHB, FEGLI, dental, vision, or other deductions have been reflected. Separate gross income from spendable income.

For Social Security, obtain an updated earnings record and estimate. For TSP, record the total balance, traditional and Roth sources, current investment allocation, outstanding loans, and beneficiary designation. A single large balance can be emotionally comforting while concealing several decisions that still need to be made.

Build the Household Balance Sheet

Federal benefits are important, but retirement happens to a household—not to a personnel file.

List bank accounts, brokerage accounts, IRAs, employer plans from prior jobs, real estate, business interests, annuities, life insurance, health savings accounts, and other meaningful assets. Then list mortgages, home-equity debt, credit cards, vehicle loans, student loans, and other obligations.

Include your spouse's assets and income sources. Couples sometimes know their combined net worth but not which account belongs to whom, how it is taxed, or what happens at the first death. Those details can change the plan.

Also identify the tax character of each account: taxable, tax-deferred, or tax-free if qualified. Two households with the same net worth can have very different retirement flexibility depending on where the money is located.

Protect the Benefits You Intend to Keep

Review your current FEHB enrollment and the record supporting your eligibility to continue coverage in retirement. In general, an employee must be enrolled—or covered as a family member—under FEHB for the five years of service immediately before retirement, or for all service since the first opportunity to enroll if less than five years. Exceptions can exist, but they should not be the plan.

Record the plan, enrollment type, covered family members, and premium. Do the same for FEGLI, FEDVIP, long-term-care coverage, and any private insurance. For FEGLI, identify the Basic and optional coverage actually in force and how cost and coverage may change after retirement.

Insurance decisions should connect to a need. Life insurance may protect a spouse, replace a survivor benefit, pay debt, create liquidity, or support a legacy. Long-term-care coverage or designated assets may protect independence. "I have insurance through work" is not yet an analysis.

A Beneficiary Audit Is Not Optional

Federal retirement benefits do not all follow one universal beneficiary form. TSP, FEGLI, unpaid compensation, and retirement contributions can involve separate designation systems and statutory orders of precedence.

Review each designation directly. Do not assume a will overrides it. Do not assume a divorce automatically repaired it. Do not assume the person you named fifteen years ago still fits the plan—or is still someone you would invite to lunch.

Marriage, divorce, remarriage, births, deaths, adoptions, estrangement, and changes in charitable intent are all reasons to review beneficiary choices. Coordinate those choices with wills, trusts, property titles, powers of attorney, and the intended survivor election.

The purpose is not merely to have a name on every form. It is to make sure the right assets reach the right people in the right way, with as little confusion as possible.

Create a What-We-Do-Not-Know List

You will probably find missing information. That is progress.

Write every uncertainty on one list: Is the military deposit fully paid? Which service date is being used for retirement? Is the high-3 estimate current? Did a prior refund affect the annuity? Can FEHB continue? Who is named on the TSP account? How much of TSP is traditional? What pension election does the spouse expect?

A vague concern creates anxiety. A written question creates an assignment.

Next to each item, identify the document, agency office, plan administrator, or qualified professional needed to resolve it. Give the question a deadline. Retirement surprises are not more charming because they arrive in an official envelope.

Your Purpose Driven Federal Employee Action Step

Create your Federal Retirement Inventory. Do not wait until every item is perfect; begin with what you have and mark what must be verified.

Federal service record Career history, significant SF-50s, retirement coverage, breaks in service, part-time or intermittent service, and a verified retirement service computation.

Deposit and redeposit questions Any civilian service, refunded contributions, or other periods that may require a decision.

Military service Discharge documents, earnings record, deposit calculation, proof of payment, and agency confirmation of credit.

Federal income estimates Pension, survivor-election effect, supplement if applicable, Social Security, and TSP—including traditional/Roth amounts and any loan.

Insurance FEHB enrollment history, FEGLI elections, FEDVIP, long-term-care protection, and private coverage.

Household balance sheet Assets, debts, account ownership, tax character, and each spouse's income sources.

Beneficiaries and estate documents Current designations for each federal benefit and financial account, coordinated with wills, trusts, titles, and powers of attorney.

What-we-do-not-know list Every unanswered question, who will resolve it, and the date by which you will follow up.

Then share the inventory with your spouse or trusted person. If your retirement plan only works when one person remembers where everything is, the plan has a single point of failure.

This inventory is your "You Are Here" dot. In the chapters ahead, we will use it to calculate what your benefits can do—and whether they are pointed toward the life you actually want.

Chapter 3

When Can You Retire?

Federal employees frequently ask one question first: "When can I retire?"

It sounds simple. It is not. In federal retirement, the word retire can mean becoming eligible for an immediate unreduced annuity, accepting a reduced annuity, leaving now and postponing the start date, separating before eligibility and applying later, accepting an agency early-out, or retiring under special provisions.

Those choices can produce very different consequences for the pension, FEHB, FEGLI, survivor protection, the FERS annuity supplement, and access to the TSP. Two employees can leave on the same Friday with the same years of service and begin very different retirements on Monday.

So the better question is: Under which retirement provision can I leave, what does it provide, and what do I give up?

Eligibility Is a Doorway, Not a Recommendation

Retirement eligibility tells you which doors the law allows you to open. It does not tell you which door leads to the life you planned.

An employee may qualify for an immediate pension and still have an income gap. Another may benefit by working a few months longer to reach a new service threshold. Someone eligible for MRA+10 may avoid a permanent reduction by postponing the annuity, but must understand what happens to health and life insurance during the postponement.

The Provision Matters

The federal retirement system does not grade decisions on enthusiasm. It applies the provision under which you retire. That is why the label attached to your separation matters nearly as much as the date.

The Standard FERS Retirement Doors

Most FERS employees qualify for an immediate, unreduced basic annuity through one of three common combinations: age 62 with at least five years of creditable civilian service; age 60 with at least twenty years; or Minimum Retirement Age with at least thirty years.

The Minimum Retirement Age—MRA—depends on year of birth. It ranges from age 55 for people born before 1948 to age 57 for people born after 1969. For those born from 1953 through 1964, it is age 56, then rises by two months per birth year from 1965 through 1969.

These are eligibility rules, not pension formulas. Reaching age 60 with twenty years may open the retirement door; it does not mean the pension replaces the paycheck. The annuity amount still depends on high-3 average salary, creditable service, the applicable multiplier, survivor election, and deductions.

Verify Before You Calculate

It is also possible to meet a threshold on paper while a service-credit issue keeps the claim from qualifying as expected. Verify the retirement SCD and every deposit or redeposit decision before treating the date as firm.

MRA+10: Available Does Not Mean Painless

FERS permits an employee who has reached the MRA and has at least ten years—but fewer than thirty—to retire under the MRA+10 provision.

If the annuity begins immediately, it is generally reduced by five percent for each year the retiree is under age 62, calculated monthly. That can be a substantial permanent haircut. Federal retirement already has enough acronyms; it does not need an accidental coupon code.

There is an important exception to the age reduction: with at least twenty years of service, an annuity that begins at age 60 or later is not reduced. With thirty years, the employee meets the regular MRA-and-30 provision.

An MRA+10 retiree is not eligible for the FERS annuity supplement. That matters when a plan assumes some form of Social Security bridge before age 62.

MRA+10 may still be the right choice. Health, family responsibilities, job satisfaction, or another opportunity may make leaving worthwhile. The point is to price the decision before making it.

Postponed Is Not the Same as Deferred

These two words are often used interchangeably in conversation. Under FERS, they describe different situations.

A postponed retirement generally applies when an employee separates after reaching the MRA with at least ten years of service and delays the beginning of the MRA+10 annuity to reduce or eliminate the age reduction. If the employee met the insurance-continuation requirements before separation, FEHB and eligible FEGLI coverage may generally be reinstated when the postponed annuity begins. Coverage does not simply continue through the waiting period.

A deferred retirement generally applies when an employee leaves federal service before qualifying for an immediate retirement and later applies for an annuity based on prior service. A former FERS employee with at least five years of creditable civilian service may generally claim at age 62; other age-and-service combinations may permit an earlier start, sometimes with a reduction.

A deferred annuity ordinarily does not restore FEHB or FEGLI. It also does not provide the FERS annuity supplement. The pension can survive the separation; some of the supporting benefits may not.

That distinction is one reason a resignation letter should not be written before the retirement provision has been identified. "I left government and can collect something later" is not the same benefit package as retiring on an immediate annuity.

Early Retirement: When the Agency Opens a Temporary Door

A Voluntary Early Retirement Authority, commonly called VERA or an early-out, allows an agency undergoing approved restructuring or downsizing to offer retirement before the usual age-and-service combinations.

The usual minimum is age 50 with at least twenty years of creditable service, or any age with at least twenty-five years. The employee must also meet the conditions of the agency's specific authorization and separate during the approved window.

Under FERS, a VERA annuity is not subject to the MRA+10 age reduction. However, "no age reduction" does not mean "no planning consequences." Leaving earlier can mean fewer years in the pension calculation, a lower high-3 than continued employment might have produced, fewer future TSP contributions and matching funds, and a longer retirement to finance.

The FERS annuity supplement may be payable to an eligible VERA retiree, but generally not until the person reaches MRA. The supplement has its own eligibility and earnings-test rules, which we will address later.

An early-out is an opportunity, not a command from the retirement gods. Evaluate the offer against the purpose, income, healthcare, and tax plan.

Discontinued Service Retirement

Discontinued Service Retirement—DSR—may apply after a qualifying involuntary separation that is not based on misconduct or delinquency. The age-and-service thresholds are generally age 50 with twenty years or any age with twenty-five years.

A DSR is different from simply disliking a reassignment, declining an acceptable position, or deciding that a reorganization feels involuntary. The nature of the personnel action and the position offered can determine eligibility.

Because the facts are agency-specific, obtain the proposed personnel action and a written benefits determination before making commitments. When your retirement depends on the precise meaning of "involuntary," this is not the moment to rely on hallway consensus.

Special-Provision Employees

Law enforcement officers, firefighters, air traffic controllers, nuclear materials couriers, certain Customs and Border Protection officers, Capitol Police, and other covered groups may be subject to special retirement provisions.

For many covered FERS law-enforcement, firefighter, and air-traffic-controller positions, eligibility can occur at age 50 with twenty years of covered service or at any age with twenty-five years of covered service. Different contribution rates, enhanced pension computations, mandatory-separation rules, and coverage definitions may apply.

The key word is covered. Working near law enforcement is not covered law-enforcement service. Having a demanding position is not automatically special-category service. The position and the service must qualify under the applicable rules, and mixed service histories require careful review.

Preserve agency certifications of covered service and verify that every qualifying period is recorded correctly. A title on an old business card is less persuasive than the retirement record.

Disability Retirement Is a Separate Protection

Disability retirement is not an early-retirement shortcut. It is a separate benefit for an employee whose medical condition prevents useful and efficient service in the position and when accommodation or reassignment requirements cannot be satisfied.

Under FERS, an employee generally needs at least eighteen months of creditable civilian service. The application normally must be filed before separation or within one year afterward, subject to a narrow exception for mental incompetence. A FERS applicant must also apply for Social Security disability benefits.

Approval standards, medical evidence, agency documentation, workers' compensation interaction, earnings limits, and later recomputation rules make this a specialized process. Anyone facing a serious medical separation should coordinate with the agency, physicians, and qualified counsel or benefits professionals early.

The planning lesson is simple: do not resign casually when illness may be ending the career. The personnel action selected today can affect the protections available tomorrow.

A Brief Word About CSRS and CSRS Offset

Most current federal employees are covered by FERS, but many households still include a CSRS or CSRS Offset employee or retiree.

The standard CSRS optional-retirement combinations are age 62 with five years, age 60 with twenty years, or age 55 with thirty years. CSRS also has early, discontinued-service, disability, deferred, and special-provision rules, but the annuity calculation and age-reduction rules differ from FERS.

CSRS Offset adds coordination with Social Security. It should not be analyzed as though it were either pure CSRS or ordinary FERS. The words "Offset" on the retirement coverage record are a request for more analysis, not a decorative subtitle.

Mixed Records Need Individual Review

This book will flag major CSRS distinctions, but a mixed CSRS/FERS or CSRS Offset record deserves an individualized calculation.

The Retirement-Date Trap

After identifying eligibility, the exact separation date still matters. FERS and CSRS have different annuity commencing-date rules. Annual-leave payout, the end of a pay period, unused sick leave, payroll processing, insurance deductions, and the agency's application timeline can also affect the transition.

There is no universally perfect day to retire. The popular date at the end of the calendar year may maximize annual-leave considerations for one employee and create an unnecessary month without annuity income for another.

Choose the date only after you know the retirement provision, annuity commencing rule, leave balances, cash-flow bridge, and processing expectations. A date should be the result of the plan—not the plan itself.

Can, Should, and Will

Before filing, answer three separate questions.

Can I retire? Identify the exact statutory provision, eligibility date, and verified service history.

Should I retire? Measure income, taxes, healthcare, survivor needs, purpose, and the value of working longer.

Will I retire? Decide whether the plan is strong enough to act on, then complete the application and implementation work.

Many federal employees remain stuck between can and will. More information can be useful, but information cannot make the decision for you. Once the facts support the life you say you want, action is what converts eligibility into retirement.

Your Purpose Driven Federal Employee Action Step

Create a one-page Retirement Eligibility Decision Sheet. Record the following:

Retirement coverage FERS, CSRS, CSRS Offset, or another system—and the SF-50 or agency record that confirms it.

Complete the Tradeoff Review

Retirement SCD The verified date used for retirement eligibility, not merely the leave SCD in Block 31.

First eligible date The earliest date under each provision that may apply.

Provision Immediate unreduced, MRA+10, postponed, deferred, VERA, DSR, disability, or special provision.

Tradeoffs Age reduction, supplement eligibility, FEHB and FEGLI consequences, survivor options, TSP access, and income gap.

Value of waiting What three, six, twelve, or twenty-four additional months would add to the pension, TSP, high-3, leave payout, or insurance eligibility.

Life cost of waiting What time, health, relationships, or opportunities would be exchanged for that improvement.

Do not circle a retirement date until every line has an answer. Then place the decision next to the retirement vision you wrote in Chapter 1.

The goal is not to retire at the first possible moment or the last defensible moment. It is to retire when the federal rules, household resources, and life you want are finally pointing in the same direction.

Chapter 4

What Will Your Pension Actually Pay?

A federal pension estimate can create a comforting moment. A number appears on the page, usually with several decimals, and suddenly retirement feels official.

Then the first retirement payment arrives and the retiree asks a very reasonable question: "Who took the rest of it?"

The answer is usually not one mysterious deduction. It is the difference between a gross annuity calculation and a retirement paycheck after survivor protection, taxes, insurance premiums, court orders, and other elections.

This chapter begins with the formula, but it will not stop there. A pension is only useful to the household in the amount, timing, and form in which it can actually be spent.

The Three Ingredients

Most federal annuity calculations begin with three ingredients: the applicable formula, the high-3 average salary, and creditable service.

Each sounds straightforward. Each contains enough fine print to keep a benefits office employed.

The formula depends on retirement coverage, age, years of service, and whether special provisions apply. The high-3 is an average of qualifying basic pay, not simply the current salary. Creditable service depends on the retirement record, deposits, refunded contributions, part-time work, military service, and unused sick leave.

An estimate is only as reliable as those inputs. Before debating whether the result is sufficient, make sure the calculation is describing the employee who is actually retiring.

The Standard FERS Formula

For a regular FERS retirement, the standard formula is generally one percent of the high-3 average salary multiplied by years and months of creditable service.

An employee who separates for retirement at age 62 or older with at least twenty years of service generally receives the enhanced 1.1 percent multiplier.

Why One-Tenth of One Percent Matters

That extra one-tenth of one percent sounds tiny until it is applied to the entire high-3 and every year of service for life. With a $120,000 high-3 and thirty years, the one-percent formula produces $36,000 per year. The 1.1-percent formula produces $39,600—a $3,600 annual difference before other adjustments.

The enhanced multiplier is based on age and service at separation for retirement. Delaying the start of a deferred annuity until age 62 does not automatically recreate the result of separating at age 62 with twenty years.

Special-provision employees can have an enhanced formula—often 1.7 percent for up to twenty covered years plus one percent for service beyond twenty. Mixed service and special categories require a separate calculation.

High-3 Does Not Mean Final Salary

The high-3 is the highest average basic pay earned during any three consecutive years of creditable service. It is often the final thirty-six months, but not always. An earlier period can be used if qualifying basic pay was higher then.

The calculation is based on rates of basic pay and the time each rate was in effect. It is not usually three December 31 salaries added together and divided by three.

Basic pay generally includes pay subject to retirement deductions, such as locality pay and certain shift or special rates. It generally excludes overtime, bonuses, cash awards, travel allowances, and other payments not treated as basic pay for retirement purposes.

This matters for employees whose total compensation is meaningfully higher than basic pay. The W-2 may be an excellent record for taxes and a poor shortcut for the high-3.

Promotions and pay increases near retirement can raise the average gradually. A raise does not become the entire high-3 on the day it appears in the paycheck. The average must live through the calendar, one day at a time—an unusual federal process that cannot be expedited with a strongly worded email.

Years, Months, and the Days That Disappear

For computation, OPM combines creditable periods of service and generally drops any remaining fraction of a month from the total. Years and full months count; leftover days do not produce a fractional annuity payment.

This is different from eligibility, where reaching a particular day can open the retirement door. It is also why the service record should be calculated precisely rather than rounded to the nearest anniversary.

Deposits, redeposits, refunded deductions, temporary service, military service, breaks, and retirement coverage changes can all alter the service used in the formula. The number of years you worked around the federal government is not necessarily the number of years in the annuity computation.

Unused Sick Leave: Valuable, but Not Magical

For an eligible immediate FERS retirement, unused sick leave can be converted into additional service for the annuity computation. It cannot be used to meet the age-and-service requirement for retirement eligibility.

In plain English, sick leave can make the check somewhat larger after you have qualified. It generally cannot get you through the door.

A full sick-leave year is represented by 2,087 hours for conversion purposes. OPM's conversion chart translates hours into months and days of service; after service is combined, remaining fractional days that do not complete a month are discarded. Sick leave is not paid as a lump sum the way annual leave generally is.

Since 2014, eligible FERS retirees receive full credit for unused sick leave in the annuity computation. Deferred retirements generally do not receive that sick-leave credit.

Using sick leave when legitimately needed is not a retirement-planning failure. Your health is not a rounding error. But an employee who reaches retirement with a large balance should make sure it appears in the calculation.

Part-Time Service Can Change the Answer

Part-time service often receives full calendar credit when determining whether an employee meets an age-and-service eligibility requirement, but the annuity computation is generally prorated to reflect the relationship between hours actually worked and the hours that would have been worked on a full-time schedule.

That distinction can surprise someone who says, correctly, "I have thirty years," but expects a pension based on thirty full-time years.

Rules can differ based on the retirement system and when the part-time service occurred, particularly for older CSRS service. Intermittent service presents additional issues. Obtain an agency estimate that identifies the part-time periods and shows the proration rather than relying on a generic online calculator.

The CSRS Formula

The standard CSRS formula is more generous than the regular FERS basic-annuity formula because CSRS was designed as a different retirement system and generally does not include the same Social Security and agency-matching structure as FERS.

The CSRS formula generally provides 1.5 percent of the high-3 for each of the first five years, 1.75 percent for each of the next five years, and two percent for each year beyond ten.

At thirty years, that produces 56.25 percent of the high-3 before reductions. The regular CSRS maximum is generally eighty percent of the high-3, reached at forty-one years and eleven months, although credit from unused sick leave can increase the result above that limit.

CSRS Offset uses a CSRS-style computation with an offset connected to Social Security eligibility. A transferee may also have separate CSRS and FERS components. These calculations should be reviewed as components, not blended into one convenient percentage.

The Survivor Election Changes the Retiree's Check

A pension estimate may show an unreduced annuity even though a married employee expects to provide a survivor benefit.

Under FERS, a full survivor election generally reduces the retiree's annuity by ten percent and can provide an eligible surviving spouse fifty percent of the unreduced annuity. A partial election generally reduces the annuity by five percent and provides twenty-five percent. A married employee generally needs spousal consent to elect less than the full benefit.

Under CSRS, the maximum survivor benefit is generally fifty-five percent of the unreduced earned annuity. The retiree reduction is calculated differently: 2.5 percent of the first $3,600 of the elected base, plus ten percent of the amount above $3,600.

The survivor election is not merely a cost. It is an insurance decision, and it may be connected to the surviving spouse's ability to continue FEHB. We will evaluate it in depth later. For this chapter, make sure the pension estimate and household income plan use the same election.

From Gross Annuity to Spendable Income

The formula produces a gross annual annuity. It does not produce the deposit that reaches the bank.

Start by dividing the annual amount by twelve. Then account for the survivor reduction, federal income-tax withholding, state tax if applicable, FEHB premiums, FEGLI premiums, FEDVIP or other deductions, court-ordered benefits, allotments, and any elected withholding.

A portion of the annuity may be treated as a tax-free recovery of the employee's after-tax retirement contributions under federal tax rules, but most retirees should expect a substantial portion of the pension to be taxable. State treatment varies widely.

Medicare Part B premiums are commonly deducted from Social Security rather than the federal annuity, but they still affect household spendable income. IRMAA can increase those premiums when income crosses applicable thresholds.

Never compare a gross pension estimate with a net working paycheck. One is before retirement deductions; the other is after payroll deductions. Put both on the same basis before deciding whether retirement income is enough.

The First Payment May Not Be the Final Payment

Federal retirement claims take time to process. OPM may issue interim payments while the claim is being adjudicated. Interim payments can be lower than the final regular annuity and may not reflect every deduction or election immediately.

A later adjustment can reconcile amounts after the final computation. That does not remove the need for a cash-flow reserve during the transition.

Build a bridge for several months of living expenses and avoid scheduling every major retirement purchase for the week after the farewell luncheon. The government may owe the correct amount eventually; the mortgage company remains oddly interested in the due date.

What One More Year Really Buys

Working another year can improve the pension in several ways. It adds service, may raise the high-3, may move the employee into the 1.1-percent FERS formula at age 62 with twenty years, and may increase unused sick leave.

Calculate the improvement in dollars, not slogans. Then compare the additional lifetime income with the year of retirement being exchanged for it.

A higher pension can be valuable. So can a healthy year. The right answer depends on whether the improvement changes the security of the plan or merely makes a good plan slightly larger.

Your Purpose Driven Federal Employee Action Step

Build a Pension Reality Check using your most recent agency estimate.

Coverage and formula Confirm FERS, CSRS, CSRS Offset, a mixed component, or a special formula.

High-3 List the dates, basic-pay rates, and assumptions used. Do not substitute current salary or total W-2 compensation.

Creditable service Reconcile civilian service, military deposits, refunds, part-time periods, and sick-leave credit.

Retirement provision Confirm whether an age reduction or different computation applies.

Complete the Net-Pension Review

Survivor election Show the unreduced annuity, elected survivor benefit, and reduction to the retiree's check.

Gross-to-net deductions Estimate federal and state taxes, FEHB, FEGLI, FEDVIP, court orders, and other withholding.

Transition reserve Identify the cash available while the claim is processed and interim payments are being made.

One-more-year comparison Calculate the pension at the preferred date and at least one later date, then identify what the additional work actually purchases.

Write the estimated monthly deposit—not merely the gross annual annuity—into the household retirement-income plan.

Your pension is a powerful benefit. Its job is not to look impressive on an estimate. Its job is to arrive in the amount your household expects and reliably support the life you are building.

Chapter 5

The Bridge to Social Security

Many FERS employees expect retirement income to arrive in a tidy three-part package: pension, Social Security, and TSP.

That description is correct in the same way that saying a car has an engine, tires, and a steering wheel is correct. It names the parts. It does not tell you when they begin, how they interact, or whether you are headed toward the life you intended.

The years between federal retirement and Social Security can be especially confusing. Some retirees receive the FERS annuity supplement. Some do not. The supplement ends at age sixty-two whether Social Security begins then or not. Social Security itself offers several claiming ages, and the choice can affect both the retiree and a surviving spouse for decades.

The objective is not to collect every check at the first possible moment. It is to build the right income bridge for the household.

The FERS Annuity Supplement Is Not Social Security

The FERS annuity supplement—often called the Special Retirement Supplement or simply the supplement—is a temporary benefit paid by OPM to certain eligible FERS retirees who leave before age sixty-two on an immediate annuity.

It is designed to approximate the portion of an age-sixty-two Social Security benefit attributable to civilian service under FERS. It is not a Social Security payment, it does not come from the Social Security Administration, and receiving it does not mean you have filed for Social Security.

Think of it as a federal bridge. The bridge may help carry eligible employees from retirement to age sixty-two. It does not decide what they should do when they reach the other side.

This distinction matters because employees sometimes build a plan that assumes the supplement will continue until they decide to claim Social Security at full retirement age or age seventy. It will not. The supplement stops at age sixty-two. If Social Security is delayed, the household must fund the gap from some other source.

Who May Receive the Supplement?

A regular FERS employee may generally qualify after retiring with an immediate, unreduced annuity at the Minimum Retirement Age with at least thirty years of service, or at age sixty with at least twenty years.

An employee who retires under an approved early-out or involuntary retirement provision may become eligible for the supplement upon reaching the Minimum Retirement Age. Special-provision employees—including certain law-enforcement officers, firefighters, and air traffic controllers—follow additional rules and may receive the supplement before MRA.

The supplement is generally not available with an MRA+10 retirement, a deferred retirement, or a disability retirement. A postponed MRA+10 annuity does not turn into a supplement-eligible retirement merely because the employee waited to start the pension.

Eligibility is tied to the retirement provision, not simply to having worked under FERS. Two employees can leave on the same day with similar service and receive different answers because they walked through different statutory retirement doors.

Before including the supplement in a retirement-income plan, confirm the retirement provision in writing. 'My coworker got it' is not a retirement provision, even if the coworker explains it with great confidence near the office coffee machine.

How the Supplement Is Estimated

The supplement is based on a Social Security-style calculation, but it is not necessarily equal to the age-sixty-two amount shown on a Social Security statement.

A common planning approximation begins with the estimated age-sixty-two Social Security benefit and multiplies it by years of FERS civilian service divided by forty. For example, an age-sixty-two estimate of $2,000 and thirty years of FERS service produces a rough supplement estimate of $1,500 per month.

That shortcut is useful for early planning, not for writing the household budget in permanent ink. OPM applies its own statutory computation, and the underlying Social Security estimate can change with earnings history and assumptions.

Service that helps the basic FERS pension does not always increase the supplement in the same way. Military service deposits, unused sick leave, and non-FERS service require careful treatment. The supplement is intended to approximate Social Security earned through covered civilian FERS service—

not to award a second Social Security history for every year that appears in the pension calculation.

The Earnings Test Can Reduce It

The supplement is subject to an annual earnings test similar to the Social Security earnings test. If wages or net earnings from self-employment exceed the applicable annual exempt amount, the supplement is generally reduced by one dollar for every two dollars above the limit.

The exempt amount changes periodically. Use the current figure for the year being planned rather than preserving an old seminar slide as if it were carved into a federal building.

The earnings test generally focuses on earned income. Pension payments, TSP withdrawals, IRA distributions, investment income, and many other forms of unearned income generally do not count as earnings for this test. They may create tax consequences, but that is a different test run by a different part of the government—because one test would apparently be too convenient.

A retiree who returns to work, consults, or starts a business should estimate the reduction before spending the full supplement. OPM uses an earnings survey to reconcile income, and overpayments can be recovered later.

Special-provision retirees can have different timing for when the earnings test begins. This is another area where the employee's exact retirement category matters.

The Age-Sixty-Two Drop-Off

The supplement ends at age sixty-two, regardless of whether the retiree claims Social Security. This creates one of the most important cash-flow decisions in federal retirement.

Suppose a retiree receives a $1,500 monthly supplement. At sixty-two, that $18,000 annual income disappears. The retiree can claim Social Security, replace the income from the TSP or another account, reduce spending, work, or combine several sources.

None of those choices is automatically wrong. The mistake is reaching sixty-two and discovering the decision when the deposit changes.

Model the household income at retirement, at age sixty-two, at Medicare eligibility, at each spouse's Social Security claiming date, when required minimum distributions begin, and after the first death. Retirement income is not one snapshot. It is a moving picture—and Uncle Sam occasionally changes the cast.

Social Security Is a Separate Decision

Eligible workers can generally begin Social Security retirement benefits as early as age sixty-two. Claiming before full retirement age permanently reduces the monthly retirement benefit. Waiting beyond full retirement age earns delayed retirement credits until age seventy.

For people born in 1960 or later, full retirement age is sixty-seven. Earlier birth years can have a different full retirement age. The correct age should be verified rather than assumed.

The supplement's expiration does not force a Social Security application. It creates an income gap. Whether claiming Social Security is the best way to fill that gap depends on health, longevity, marital status, survivor needs, employment, taxes, investment resources, and the purpose assigned to other assets.

Federal retirement and Social Security are adjacent decisions, not a package deal.

Your Estimate Is Built From Thirty-Five Years

Social Security retirement benefits are generally based on the highest thirty-five years of indexed covered earnings. If fewer than thirty-five years are available, zeros can be included in the calculation.

Most FERS civilian earnings are covered by Social Security and can help build that record. Traditional CSRS service generally was not covered, although many CSRS employees also earned Social Security credits through other work or had CSRS Offset service.

Working longer can replace a zero or a lower earnings year. In other cases, another year has only a modest effect because the worker already has thirty-five stronger years. Review the earnings record itself. A missing or incorrect year can affect the calculation, and retirement is an expensive time to discover that a former employer and a database had creative differences.

The Social Security estimate should also reflect the intended stopping date. An online estimate that assumes continued earnings until a future claiming age may overstate the benefit for someone planning to retire from federal service years earlier.

WEP and GPO Were Repealed

For years, federal retirement education warned CSRS and other public-sector employees about the Windfall Elimination Provision and Government Pension Offset. Those rules could reduce a worker's Social Security retirement benefit or a spouse's Social Security benefit because of a pension from non-covered employment.

The Social Security Fairness Act, signed into law on January 5, 2025, repealed WEP and GPO for benefits payable for January 2024 and later.

That is a major change. Older books, benefit estimates, seminar materials, and well-meaning hallway advice may still describe reductions that no longer apply.

Repeal does not mean every CSRS retiree automatically qualifies for Social Security. A person still needs the required covered work credits and must meet the applicable eligibility rules. It means the former WEP and GPO reductions no longer apply to benefits payable for the affected period.

Break-Even Is a Tool, Not a Strategy

A break-even calculation asks how long a person must live for larger delayed benefits to catch up with benefits collected earlier. It can be useful. It is not a complete claiming strategy.

Break-even analysis often ignores taxes, investment returns, spending needs, employment, Medicare premiums, survivor benefits, and the emotional value of dependable lifetime income. It can also treat a married couple as two unrelated spreadsheets who happen to share a kitchen.

Social Security is longevity insurance. The longer a retiree lives, the more valuable a larger inflation-adjusted lifetime benefit can become. For a married couple, delaying the higher earner's benefit can also strengthen the income eventually available to the surviving spouse.

The objective is not to win a private contest against Social Security. The objective is to protect the retirement plan under the circumstances the household may actually face.

Married Couples Should Plan Two Lives—and One

While both spouses are alive, the household may receive two Social Security benefits. After the first death, the surviving spouse generally receives one benefit—the survivor benefit rules can allow the larger applicable amount, but the two checks do not continue side by side.

That makes the higher earner's claiming decision especially important. Delaying that benefit can increase the worker's lifetime payment and may increase the survivor benefit later.

One useful approach is staging: the spouse with the smaller benefit may claim earlier to create income while the higher earner delays, when the broader plan supports it. The household receives some income now while strengthening the larger lifetime benefit for the future survivor.

Staging is not automatically right for every couple. Health, age differences, work plans, cash flow, and benefit eligibility matter. But it demonstrates why 'we both claim at sixty-two' and 'we both wait until seventy' are not the only choices.

Working After Claiming Has Its Own Earnings Test

Social Security retirement benefits claimed before full retirement age can also be withheld when earned income exceeds the applicable limit. Different rules apply in the year full retirement age is reached, and the earnings test no longer applies beginning with the month full retirement age is attained.

Benefits withheld under the Social Security earnings test are not simply lost forever. At full retirement age, Social Security adjusts the benefit to account for months in which benefits were withheld. Even so, the temporary cash-flow effect can be substantial.

Do not confuse the Social Security earnings test with the FERS supplement earnings test. They are separate benefits administered by separate agencies. A retiree can encounter one, the other, both at different times, or neither.

Taxes Can Change the Best Claiming Date

Social Security does not exist outside the tax plan. Depending on combined income, up to eighty-five percent of Social Security benefits may be included in federal taxable income. That does not mean an eighty-five-percent tax rate; it means up to eighty-five percent of the benefit enters the tax calculation.

Claiming decisions can affect the years available for Roth conversions, capital-gain realization, TSP withdrawals, and other income planning. Later, required minimum distributions can add taxable income whether or not the retiree needs the money for spending.

Medicare's income-related monthly adjustment amount—our old friend Auntie IRMAA—can also make higher income more expensive. Because IRMAA generally uses tax-return information from two years earlier, a decision made today can arrive later wearing a Medicare nametag.

The best Social Security age cannot be selected in isolation from the TSP and tax strategy. We will return to that interaction in depth.

Why Specialized Federal Guidance Matters

Federal retirement decisions sit at the intersection of OPM rules, Social Security rules, taxes, investments, insurance, and household goals. A correct answer in one system can still create a poor result in the complete plan.

That is why specialized education matters. The Chartered Federal Employee Benefits Consultant℠—ChFEBC℠—designation provides financial professionals with focused training in federal employee benefits and the planning issues surrounding them. Social Security-specific education, such as the National Social Security Advisor credential, adds another layer when claiming and survivor decisions are involved.

A designation is not a substitute for judgment, and no credential guarantees a good plan. It does, however, signal that the professional has invested in understanding rules that many general financial conversations barely touch.

Federal employees do not need someone who merely recognizes the acronyms. They need someone who understands how the acronyms behave when they all show up in the same retirement.

Your Purpose Driven Federal Employee Action Step

Build a Social Security Bridge Map before choosing a claiming age.

Supplement eligibility Confirm whether your retirement provision qualifies and when payments are expected to begin.

Supplement estimate Obtain an agency estimate and identify which service was included in the computation.

Earnings exposure Estimate wages or self-employment income after retirement and test whether the supplement could be reduced.

Age-sixty-two gap Write down the monthly income that disappears when the supplement ends and identify the source that will replace it.

Complete the Household Review

Social Security record Review both the earnings history and estimates at age sixty-two, full retirement age, and age seventy.

Household claiming options Compare early, full-retirement-age, delayed, and staged strategies for both spouses.

Survivor income Recalculate household income after the first death using one Social Security benefit and the elected federal survivor annuity.

Tax coordination Compare claiming dates with planned TSP withdrawals, Roth conversions, required minimum distributions, and Medicare IRMAA exposure.

Choose the strategy that best supports the household—not merely the age that produces the most attractive answer in a break-even calculator.

The supplement is temporary. Social Security can last a lifetime. The bridge between them should be designed with the same care as the retirement waiting on the other side.

Chapter 6

Give Your TSP a Retirement Job

During a federal career, the TSP has a wonderfully simple assignment: money goes in, investments hopefully grow, and the employee tries not to panic every time the market appears on the evening news.

Retirement changes the assignment.

The TSP may now need to provide monthly income, bridge the years before Social Security, fund large purchases, create tax flexibility, cover a future long-term-care need, support a surviving spouse, and eventually pass to beneficiaries.

Those are different jobs. Treating the entire balance as one large pile labeled 'retirement' does not tell you how the money should be invested or withdrawn.

A TSP balance is not a retirement-income plan. It is a resource waiting for instructions.

Accumulation and Distribution Are Different Games

While working, contributions and time can help an employee recover from a market decline. In retirement, withdrawals reverse the direction of cash flow. Selling during a decline can lock in losses and leave fewer shares available for a later recovery.

This is sequence-of-returns risk. Two retirees can earn the same average return over a long period and experience very different outcomes because one suffered losses while taking withdrawals early in retirement.

That does not mean the TSP should be moved entirely to the G Fund on retirement day. A retirement that lasts thirty years still needs growth. Inflation remains employed even after you are not.

The better question is not, 'Which fund is safest?' It is, 'Which dollars will be needed soon, which dollars must grow, and which dollars have another purpose?'

The TSP Funds Still Need Jobs

The G Fund invests in special Treasury securities and offers a combination that is difficult to duplicate outside the TSP: government-backed principal stability with an interest rate based on longer-term Treasury securities. That can make it useful for liquidity and near-term spending.

The F Fund provides broad U.S. bond-market exposure and can fluctuate as interest rates and credit markets change. The C Fund tracks large U.S. companies, the S Fund covers U.S. companies outside the C Fund, and the I Fund provides international stock exposure under its applicable benchmark.

Lifecycle Funds combine underlying TSP funds and adjust the mix over time. They can be a reasonable all-in-one allocation, but the year in the fund's name is not a personalized retirement plan. It does not know about your pension, spouse, taxes, house, long-term-care concern, or strong preference for taking the entire family on a cruise every other summer.

The mutual fund window expands investment choice for eligible participants but adds rules, fees, and complexity. More choices do not automatically produce more planning.

Your Main Choices After Separation

A separated participant generally has several ways to use the TSP. The options can be combined rather than treated as an all-or-nothing election.

You may leave money invested in the TSP. You may request partial distributions, installment payments, or a total distribution. You may roll eligible money to an IRA or another eligible employer plan. You may use part or all of an eligible balance to purchase a life annuity through the TSP's annuity provider.

The current distribution system can also allow a participant with traditional and Roth balances to choose the source of a withdrawal or use both proportionally, subject to TSP rules. That source decision creates useful tax-planning flexibility.

Do not select an option because it is listed first on a website or because someone at the retirement luncheon used it. Choose the combination that performs the jobs in your plan.

Reasons to Keep Money in the TSP

The TSP offers low administrative and investment expenses, institutional funds, straightforward diversification, and access to the G Fund. It also has federal-plan creditor protections and a familiar administrative structure.

Keeping at least part of the account can be particularly valuable for someone who wants the G Fund or may need the plan's special early-distribution rules.

Simplicity has value. An employee does not receive bonus retirement points for collecting seven custodians, eleven statements, and a password notebook thick enough to stop a door.

But low cost is not the only consideration. Investment selection, withdrawal control, beneficiary planning, tax strategy, service, advice, consolidation, and the household's other accounts also matter.

A Rollover Is Not Automatically an Upgrade

An IRA can provide broader investment choices, different income tools, more customized withdrawal management, and potentially more flexible beneficiary and charitable planning. It can also introduce advisory fees, product expenses, trading costs, surrender restrictions, and investment risks that were not present in the TSP.

A direct rollover of eligible pretax TSP money to a traditional IRA generally preserves tax deferral. A rollover of eligible Roth TSP money should be directed to the appropriate Roth account. Sending money to the wrong destination can create taxes and paperwork with impressive speed.

Before rolling over, compare the TSP with the actual proposed alternative—not with a brochure containing mountains, sailboats, and unusually relaxed retirees.

Document what improves, what gets worse, what costs change, what guarantees apply, what liquidity remains, and who will help manage the strategy after the rollover.

Do Not Accidentally Roll Away Early Access

The tax rules for accessing a workplace plan can differ from the rules for an IRA. A separated employee who leaves federal service during or after the calendar year in which age fifty-five is reached may qualify for an exception to the ten-percent additional tax on eligible TSP distributions. Qualified public-safety employees can have an earlier exception under applicable rules, including provisions tied to age fifty or twenty-five years of service.

The exception applies to the plan associated with the separation. Rolling the entire TSP to an IRA can eliminate access to the workplace-plan exception because an IRA follows its own penalty rules.

This does not mean the money should never be rolled over. It means an employee retiring before age fifty-nine and one-half should design the income bridge before moving the account.

Other exceptions, including substantially equal periodic payments under Section 72(t), have strict rules and consequences if modified improperly. Early-retirement access deserves individualized tax review, not an online shortcut and a hopeful expression.

Traditional and Roth Dollars Are Not Interchangeable

Traditional TSP contributions and earnings are generally tax-deferred and taxable when distributed. Qualified Roth TSP distributions are generally free of federal income tax when the applicable age and five-year requirements are met.

The labels describe tax treatment, not investment choice. Traditional and Roth balances can generally be invested in the same TSP funds. A retiree can be conservative or aggressive in either tax bucket.

Since 2024, Roth balances in employer plans such as the TSP are not subject to lifetime required minimum distributions for the original participant. Traditional balances remain subject to the applicable RMD rules.

The withdrawal source can change taxable income, Medicare IRMAA exposure, capital-gain brackets, taxation of Social Security, and the amount left in each tax bucket for later years.

The New Roth Conversion Opportunity

Beginning in 2026, the TSP allows eligible participants to convert traditional TSP money to Roth money inside the plan. The converted amount is generally included in taxable income for the year of conversion.

Because the money remains inside the account, the TSP does not withhold part of an in-plan conversion for taxes. The participant needs outside funds to pay the resulting tax and may need estimated payments or adjusted withholding.

The ability to convert does not mean the entire traditional balance should be converted at once. Large conversions can push income into higher tax brackets, increase Medicare IRMAA later, affect credits and deductions, and create a tax bill capable of turning a promising strategy into an expensive anecdote.

Conversions should be modeled across multiple years alongside pension income, Social Security, capital gains, deductions, RMDs, and the surviving spouse's future tax brackets.

The 'We'll Save It for Later' Tax Trap

Many federal retirees say they do not plan to use much of the TSP for ordinary income. They want to preserve it for a future long-term-care need or leave it to their children. The intention is admirable. The tax strategy often is not.

A large traditional TSP balance does not remain quietly tax-deferred forever. Required minimum distributions can force taxable income later, even when the retiree does not need the money for spending. Those distributions can increase marginal taxes and Medicare IRMAA exposure.

After the first spouse dies, the survivor may file as a single taxpayer while receiving much of the same pension, the larger Social Security benefit, and future RMDs. The household can lose both a person and a tax bracket.

For many nonspouse beneficiaries, inherited pretax retirement money must be distributed within ten years under current law. The distributions can arrive during the beneficiary's peak earning years and are generally taxed as ordinary income. Pretax retirement accounts can therefore be among the least tax-efficient assets to leave to children.

Preserving the TSP balance is not the same as preserving its after-tax value. Long-term-care and legacy goals should be funded with a strategy that considers the eventual tax collector too.

Installments Can Create a Retirement Paycheck

TSP installments can be used to send a recurring payment to the household. Depending on current plan rules, participants can select payment frequency and amount and may adjust or stop installments.

This can recreate the rhythm of a paycheck while the remaining balance stays invested. Partial distributions can fund occasional needs, and eligible direct rollovers can move selected amounts for other planning purposes.

The payment amount should be coordinated with the portfolio allocation. Taking monthly withdrawals from an account invested for long-term growth without a reserve can force sales during a market decline.

A distribution method answers how money leaves the account. It does not answer whether the withdrawal rate is sustainable, tax-efficient, or connected to the life the retiree wants.

The 'TSP Annuity' Is Not Actually the TSP

The name 'TSP annuity' makes the option sound like another feature maintained inside the Thrift Savings Plan. That is not what happens.

The Federal Retirement Thrift Investment Board has an exclusive arrangement with Metropolitan Life Insurance Company—MetLife—to provide the annuity. When the purchase is completed, the money used for the annuity leaves the TSP and purchases a life annuity contract from MetLife.

The TSP says this plainly: once purchased, the annuity is no longer part of the TSP account. The participant cannot change or cancel the purchase.

That is not a minor administrative detail. It is the central economic decision.

What Annuitization Actually Means

Annuitization is the conversion of a lump sum into a contractual stream of payments based on the option selected. In the TSP version, the participant gives the premium and control of those dollars to the insurance company in exchange for the promised income.

The payment can be structured around one life or joint lives and may include features such as a survivor percentage, cash-refund provision, or period-certain protection. Each protection generally reduces the starting income because the insurer may be required to pay longer or return more value.

Once annuitized, the premium is not an account balance available for a new roof, a family emergency, a better investment opportunity, long-term care, or a change of heart. The retiree owns the contractual payment—not a liquid pool of the original TSP dollars.

If the retiree dies early, the value received by heirs depends entirely on the payout option chosen. A life-only option can provide the highest starting payment but may stop at death. Refund, period-certain, and joint-life features can protect others, but at the cost of lower income.

Why the TSP Annuity Is Usually a Poor Fit

For most federal retirees I encounter, the TSP annuity's permanent loss of control creates more problems than it solves. Federal employees already have a pension and Social Security—two sources designed to provide lifetime income. Turning a large additional pool of liquid retirement savings into another irrevocable payment can leave the household asset-rich on paper and flexibility-poor in real life.

The retiree may need access for healthcare, long-term care, housing, family support, or opportunities that do not arrive in monthly installments. Inflation can erode a level payment, while available increasing-payment choices may still not match actual inflation. Death-benefit protections reduce the income and remain limited to the elected structure.

There can be exceptions. Someone who places the highest value on simple lifetime income, has substantial liquidity elsewhere, has limited legacy goals, and fully understands the irrevocable trade may find the option useful.

But it should be evaluated as an irreversible insurance purchase from MetLife—not accepted as the default 'safe' way to keep money in the TSP.

This Does Not Mean Annuities Are Bad

Annuity is a category, not a single product. Saying 'annuities are bad' is like saying 'vehicles are bad' because a school bus is difficult to parallel park.

There are immediate-income annuities, deferred-income annuities, fixed annuities, fixed-indexed annuities, variable annuities, and registered index-linked annuities. Contracts can be designed for accumulation, principal protection, market participation, lifetime income, long-term-care leverage, or legacy benefits. Costs, risks, liquidity, guarantees, and complexity vary enormously.

Most deferred annuity contracts commonly used in planning today permit withdrawals, and many offer guaranteed lifetime-withdrawal benefits without requiring formal annuitization. In those designs, income may be taken under a rider while a contract value remains available, subject to the contract's withdrawal limits, surrender schedule, market adjustments, fees, and other terms.

That flexibility is fundamentally different from surrendering the premium through irrevocable annuitization.

It does not make every modern annuity appropriate. It means the word 'annuity' alone tells us almost nothing about whether the tool is good or bad.

Judge the Contract by the Job

A powerful annuity can solve a specific planning problem. A poorly matched annuity can create costs, restrictions, and disappointment. The same is true of investments, insurance, real estate, and boats—although boats have better vacation photographs.

Ask what risk is being transferred to the insurance company. Is the objective lifetime income, protection from market loss, tax deferral, long-term-care leverage, or a death benefit? Then identify the cost, liquidity, surrender period, income calculation, insurer strength, beneficiary terms, and what happens if the plan changes.

Guarantees depend on the claims-paying ability of the issuing insurer. Income riders may have separate benefit bases that are not cash values. Index credits may be limited by caps, participation rates, spreads, or other formulas. Variable and registered products can expose the owner to market losses.

A contract should be selected because its guarantees and limitations fit a defined job—not because a salesperson described it as both completely safe and capable of performing miracles.

Build the TSP Around Time Horizons

One practical approach is to divide the TSP and related accounts by purpose and time horizon.

Money needed soon may be assigned to cash-like or lower-volatility resources. Money needed later can remain positioned for growth. Money intended for taxes, Roth conversions, healthcare, or legacy can be managed according to those separate objectives.

The divisions do not require physically opening a new account for every goal. They require knowing how much money has each job, where it is invested, and which source will be used when the job arrives.

The TSP can remain part of that system. It does not have to be the entire system.

Your Purpose Driven Federal Employee Action Step

Create a TSP Job Description before submitting a distribution or rollover request.

Near-term income Identify the monthly amount the TSP must provide during the first five years of retirement.

Age-based access Confirm whether the age-fifty-five or public-safety exception applies before moving money to an IRA.

Investment assignments Separate liquidity, intermediate spending, and long-term-growth dollars.

Tax sources Map planned withdrawals from traditional and Roth balances and model potential conversions.

Complete the Distribution Review

RMD exposure Project required distributions and the possible effect on taxes and Medicare IRMAA.

Long-term care Determine whether preserving a large pretax balance is actually the most efficient way to fund the goal.

Legacy Estimate what beneficiaries may keep after income taxes and inherited-account distribution rules.

Annuity comparison If guaranteed income is desired, compare the MetLife TSP annuity with other income tools, including liquidity, death benefits, inflation treatment, costs, and whether annuitization is required.

Keep-versus-rollover review Document the exact benefits, protections, costs, services, and limitations on both sides before transferring anything.

Do not ask the TSP to do everything. Give each dollar a job, preserve the flexibility your household may need, and make every distribution serve the retirement you said you wanted.

Chapter 7

FEHB, Medicare, and the Cost of Staying Healthy

Federal employees often describe FEHB as one of the best benefits they have. They are usually right.

Unfortunately, 'I get to keep FEHB' is sometimes treated as a complete healthcare plan. It is not. It is an eligibility statement followed by several decisions, multiple premiums, coordination rules, tax consequences, and at least one annual brochure apparently written for people who enjoy recreational fine print.

Healthcare planning in federal retirement begins with protecting the right to continue coverage. It then requires choosing the right FEHB or PSHB plan, coordinating Medicare, estimating premiums and out-of-pocket costs, protecting a surviving spouse, and preparing for care that ordinary health insurance does not cover.

Good coverage is valuable. Understanding how it works is what makes it useful.

The Five-Year Rule Is the First Gate

To continue FEHB into retirement, an employee generally must retire on an immediate annuity and have been continuously enrolled—or covered as a family member—during the five years of service immediately before retirement. If the employee had fewer than five years of service since the first opportunity to enroll, coverage generally must extend from that first opportunity.

The five years are about continuous coverage, not five years in the same plan or enrollment type. An employee may change among eligible FEHB plans and may move between Self Only, Self Plus One, and Self and Family while maintaining coverage.

Coverage under a spouse's FEHB enrollment can count. That can be important when two federal employees coordinate which spouse carries the family plan.

The requirement should be verified before separation. A waiver may exist in limited circumstances, but a retirement plan should not depend on convincing OPM that an avoidable enrollment gap deserves mercy.

Immediate, Postponed, and Deferred Matter Again

As we saw with retirement eligibility, the door used to leave federal service matters.

An employee who retires on an eligible immediate annuity and satisfies the coverage requirement can generally continue FEHB as an annuitant. An employee who leaves and later claims a deferred annuity generally cannot carry FEHB into retirement.

A properly postponed MRA+10 annuity can allow eligible FEHB coverage to resume when the annuity begins, if the employee met the applicable enrollment requirement before separation. Coverage during the postponement gap must come from another source.

The words postponed and deferred sound like cousins. In federal benefits, they can behave more like cousins who share a last name and disagree about everything else.

Retirees Still Pay Premiums

FEHB does not become free in retirement. The government generally continues contributing toward the premium, and the annuitant pays the enrollee share through the pension when possible.

The retiree usually pays premiums with after-tax dollars rather than through the premium-conversion treatment available to many active employees. That can make the net cost feel higher even when the published enrollee premium is similar.

Premiums change, plan benefits change, provider networks change, prescription formularies change, and the household's health changes. The plan that was ideal at retirement may not be ideal five years later.

Open Season is not merely the annual period when brochures reproduce in the mailbox. It is an opportunity to compare total expected cost and coverage.

Self Plus One Is Not Automatically Cheaper

A married couple may assume Self Plus One must cost less than Self and Family because it covers fewer people. Sometimes it does. In some plans or years, it may not.

Compare the actual premium for each enrollment code. Also consider whether adult children remain eligible, whether each spouse has independent federal coverage rights, and how the enrollment would function after a death or divorce.

The least expensive premium can still produce the highest total cost if deductibles, copayments, coinsurance, prescriptions, or out-of-network care are materially worse.

Healthcare math has a sense of humor. It simply does not have a particularly kind one.

The Survivor Annuity and FEHB Are Connected

For a surviving spouse to continue FEHB after an annuitant's death, the survivor generally must be eligible for a survivor annuity and have been covered under the enrollment at death.

This makes the federal survivor election more than a pension-income decision. Electing no survivor annuity can jeopardize the spouse's ability to continue FEHB, even when the couple believes other assets can replace the lost pension income.

In some situations, a survivor benefit can be structured at a reduced level while preserving FEHB eligibility. The rules, consent requirements, and household economics should be reviewed before the retirement application is signed.

A life-insurance policy or large TSP balance may replace income. It does not automatically replace eligibility for the federal health plan.

Medicare Does Not Replace FEHB Automatically

At age sixty-five, most federal annuitants become eligible for Medicare. FEHB generally continues whether or not a nonpostal annuitant enrolls in Medicare.

Medicare Part A primarily covers inpatient hospital services. Part B covers physicians, outpatient services, preventive care, durable medical equipment, and other medical services. Part D provides prescription-drug coverage. Medicare Advantage—Part C—delivers Medicare benefits through an approved private plan and often includes drug coverage and additional benefits.

FEHB and Medicare can work together. For retired federal employees, Medicare generally pays first for Medicare-covered services and FEHB pays according to its coordination rules. The order can reduce deductibles, copayments, and coinsurance, but the result depends on the particular FEHB plan.

An active employee's FEHB coverage generally pays first, which is one reason someone working past sixty-five may delay Part B. Employment status matters more than the birthday cake.

Part A Is Usually the Easy Decision

Most federal employees and annuitants qualify for premium-free Medicare Part A based on covered work. When Part A has no premium, OPM generally advises enrolling because it can reduce out-of-pocket costs and coordinate with FEHB.

There can be special considerations for someone contributing to a health savings account. Enrollment in any part of Medicare generally ends HSA contribution eligibility, and retroactive Part A coverage can create problems for late enrollees. HSA users should coordinate enrollment timing with tax guidance.

For most other retirees, premium-free Part A is the least controversial Medicare decision. Part B is where the family meeting usually gets louder.

Part B Is a Cost-Benefit Decision

Medicare Part B requires a monthly premium. Higher-income beneficiaries can pay an additional income-related amount. A retiree who keeps FEHB and enrolls in Part B is paying for two layers of coverage.

That can be worthwhile. Many FEHB plans waive or reduce cost sharing when Medicare is primary. Some provide Part B premium reimbursements or enhanced benefits for Medicare-enrolled members. Part B can also expand provider access for an annuitant enrolled in an FEHB HMO when the provider accepts Medicare.

But the value varies by plan, health usage, prescriptions, travel, provider preferences, and income. A healthy retiree with a high Part B premium may view the trade differently from someone expecting frequent outpatient care.

Do not compare only the Part B premium. Compare the combined FEHB and Medicare premiums with expected deductibles, copayments, coinsurance, prescriptions, provider access, and worst-case exposure.

Skipping Part B Has Consequences

Nonpostal FEHB annuitants generally are not required to enroll in Part B to keep FEHB. That flexibility is valuable, but it does not guarantee a consequence-free opportunity to enroll years later.

The Medicare Special Enrollment Period is generally tied to coverage based on current employment—your own or a spouse's. Retiree FEHB coverage is not current-employment coverage for this purpose.

Someone who delays Part B after retiring may face enrollment timing restrictions and a late-enrollment penalty if no Special Enrollment Period applies. The Part B penalty generally adds ten percent of the standard premium for each full twelve-month period enrollment was delayed, and it can last as long as the person has Part B.

The decision can still be reasonable in a particular plan. It simply should be made with an understanding of the future door, not only today's premium.

Part D and FEHB Drug Coverage

FEHB plans provide creditable prescription-drug coverage. An annuitant who maintains FEHB generally can defer separate Part D enrollment without the Part D late-enrollment penalty.

Some FEHB and PSHB plans offer Medicare Part D drug benefits through an employer-group arrangement for Medicare-eligible annuitants. These integrations can provide Part D protections and additional coverage while remaining connected to the federal plan.

Review notices carefully before opting out. Prescription formularies, pharmacy networks, prior-authorization rules, out-of-pocket limits, and the treatment of drugs outside the standard Part D benefit can differ.

Prescription coverage is one area where yesterday's excellent plan can become tomorrow's expensive surprise because one medication moved to a different tier.

Postal Employees Have a Different System

Beginning in 2025, eligible Postal Service employees and annuitants receive coverage through the Postal Service Health Benefits Program rather than ordinary FEHB enrollment.

PSHB resembles FEHB in many ways, but Medicare Part B rules are materially different. Certain Medicare-eligible Postal Service annuitants and family members must enroll in Part B to maintain PSHB coverage, subject to statutory exceptions.

Exceptions include certain people who retired on or before January 1, 2025, certain employees who were age sixty-four or older on January 1, 2025, and qualifying individuals based on residence outside the United States or eligibility for specified VA or Indian Health Service benefits. The precise exception must be verified.

Postal employees should never assume that general FEHB advice applies unchanged. The acronym changed because some of the rules did too.

Original Medicare or Medicare Advantage

A Medicare-eligible retiree can generally receive Part A and Part B benefits through Original Medicare or choose a Medicare Advantage plan, subject to eligibility and service-area rules.

Some FEHB plans offer a connected Medicare Advantage option for enrolled annuitants. In that arrangement, the retiree generally keeps FEHB and follows the plan's instructions rather than suspending coverage.

An annuitant who enrolls in an outside Medicare Advantage plan may, under applicable rules, be able to suspend FEHB. Suspension preserves a potential route back to FEHB. Cancellation generally does not.

Do not confuse suspend with cancel. One can preserve a return path; the other may close the door permanently. This is not the place to select whichever button appears closest to the cursor.

Never Casually Cancel FEHB

An annuitant who voluntarily cancels FEHB generally cannot reenroll later unless a limited exception applies. Suspension for qualifying coverage such as a Medicare Advantage plan, TRICARE, or Medicaid follows specific procedures and may permit reenrollment.

Before changing coverage, obtain the retirement system's instructions and confirm the exact status in writing. Do not simply stop a payment or tell a carrier that coverage is no longer wanted.

The right to return to FEHB can be more valuable than a short-term premium difference. It is an option that should not be surrendered accidentally.

Auntie IRMAA Joins the Appointment

Medicare Part B and Part D premiums can increase when modified adjusted gross income exceeds annual thresholds. The income-related monthly adjustment amount—IRMAA—is determined separately for each Medicare beneficiary.

IRMAA generally uses tax information from two years earlier. A large TSP distribution, Roth conversion, capital gain, or other income event can therefore raise Medicare premiums later, after the check from the transaction has stopped feeling exciting.

The thresholds are cliffs. Even a modest amount of income over a threshold can place the beneficiary into the next premium tier for the year.

This is why federal employees who plan to preserve pretax TSP money indefinitely need a long-range tax projection. RMDs can create taxable income and Medicare costs whether the retiree needs the distribution or not.

Retirement Can Support an IRMAA Appeal

The first IRMAA determination after retirement may be based on a tax return from a high-earning working year. Work stoppage or work reduction can qualify as a life-changing event for requesting a new determination based on lower, more current income.

Social Security uses Form SSA-44 and supporting information for this request. Retirement does not automatically erase IRMAA; the beneficiary must act.

An appeal should use a reasonable income estimate that includes pension income, taxable distributions, conversions, capital gains, interest, dividends, and the other items entering the applicable Medicare income calculation.

Underestimating income to reduce a premium is not planning. It is scheduling an unpleasant follow-up letter.

FEHB Is Not Long-Term-Care Insurance

FEHB and Medicare cover medical care. They generally do not pay for extended custodial care simply because a person needs help with activities of daily living.

Long-term care may be provided at home, in assisted living, in an adult-care setting, or in a nursing facility. The cost can threaten the surviving spouse's lifestyle and consume assets originally intended for income or legacy.

A plan may use personal assets, insurance, hybrid life or annuity benefits, family support, public benefits, or a combination. The right solution depends on health, age, assets, cash flow, family, and purpose.

Keeping a large traditional TSP balance 'for long-term care' can create RMDs and taxes for years before care is needed. The asset should be evaluated on an after-tax basis and compared with other ways to fund or leverage the risk.

Plan for Two Healthcare Timelines

Spouses rarely reach Medicare eligibility, retire, or need care on the same date. One may be an active employee while the other is an annuitant. One may have Medicare while the other remains covered only by FEHB. One may use far more healthcare than the other.

Build the plan year by year. Identify who is working, which coverage is primary, who has Part A, who has Part B, which enrollment tier applies, and what the household pays after taxes.

Then model the first death. Confirm the survivor annuity, FEHB continuation, Medicare premiums, IRMAA filing status, and the income available to pay healthcare costs.

The goal is not merely to have insurance cards. It is to preserve access to care without sacrificing the retirement those cards were meant to protect.

Your Purpose Driven Federal Employee Action Step

Build a Federal Healthcare Timeline for both spouses.

Continuation eligibility Confirm the immediate-annuity requirement and document five years of FEHB or qualifying family-member coverage.

Survivor protection Verify that the planned survivor election preserves FEHB eligibility for the spouse.

Enrollment tier Compare Self Only, Self Plus One, and Self and Family premiums and coverage needs.

Plan comparison Review annual premiums, deductibles, copayments, coinsurance, prescriptions, networks, travel coverage, and maximum exposure.

Medicare dates List each spouse's Part A and Part B eligibility and any Special Enrollment Period deadline.

Complete the Medicare Coordination Review

Part B analysis Compare combined premiums and IRMAA with the cost sharing, reimbursements, and provider access available under the FEHB or PSHB plan.

Postal rules If applicable, document whether each Medicare-eligible family member is subject to the PSHB Part B requirement or qualifies for an exception.

IRMAA projection Model income two years ahead and identify whether an SSA-44 request may be appropriate after retirement.

Long-term care Separate ordinary medical coverage from the plan for extended custodial care.

Do-not-cancel warning Before leaving FEHB or PSHB, confirm whether the action is an approved suspension with reenrollment rights or a permanent cancellation.

Healthcare coverage is not a box to check once. Protect the eligibility, coordinate the payers, review the plan annually, and make sure both spouses know what happens next.

Chapter 8

The Tax Window You May Never Get Back

Federal employees are trained to accumulate benefits. Put money into the TSP. Earn the pension. Protect FEHB. Build sick leave. Reach the service date.

Then retirement arrives, and the tax code introduces a new assignment: decide which income to recognize, from which account, in which year, under which filing status, before several government programs begin reacting to the same tax return.

Many retirees respond by taking only what they need and leaving the traditional TSP untouched. It feels conservative. It can also allow a future tax problem to compound quietly in the background.

Tax planning is not about paying nothing. It is about deciding when, where, and by whom taxes are paid so that more of the money supports the people and purposes for which it was saved.

Tax Preparation Records the Past

Tax preparation answers, 'What happened last year, and how do we report it correctly?' Tax planning asks, 'What can we do before December 31 to improve this year and the years that follow?'

Both matter. They are not the same service.

A return can be perfectly prepared after a poor tax decision. The form may be accurate, the math may be flawless, and the result may still include a preventable bracket increase, avoidable IRMAA, or a missed conversion opportunity.

Retirement creates choices that payroll withholding often concealed. The household now controls distributions, conversions, capital gains, charitable transfers, and sometimes the timing of Social Security. That control is valuable only when used before the year closes.

Your Federal Pension Is Mostly Taxable

FERS and CSRS annuity payments are generally subject to federal income tax. Because employee retirement contributions were made with after-tax dollars, a portion of each payment may represent a tax-free recovery of that cost.

For most modern federal retirees, OPM determines the taxable and tax-free portions using the Simplified Method and reports the annuity on Form CSA 1099-R. The tax-free portion is usually much smaller than the retiree imagines.

A $50,000 pension is not automatically $50,000 of taxable income, but it is also not a tax-free return of decades of service. Most of the payment should generally be expected to enter the federal tax calculation.

Survivor annuities have their own reporting and recovery rules. Review the tax form rather than copying last year's percentage forever.

Traditional TSP Money Has a Silent Partner

Traditional TSP contributions generally reduced taxable income when made, and growth accumulated tax-deferred. The bargain was deferral—not forgiveness.

When pretax money is distributed, the taxable amount is generally ordinary income. The government does not own a fixed percentage of the account because the future tax rate is unknown. Its share depends on the law, the size and timing of distributions, other income, filing status, and where the retiree lives.

A $1 million traditional TSP statement does not mean the household owns $1 million of spendable value. It owns the account subject to a future tax claim.

This is why pretax and Roth balances should never be compared dollar for dollar without considering taxes. One is a gross amount. The other may be much closer to spendable value when distribution requirements are satisfied.

The 'Save It for Long-Term Care' Problem

Many federal retirees intend to preserve the traditional TSP for a future long-term-care need. The goal is prudent. The method can be inefficient.

The account may continue growing while required distributions eventually force taxable income. Those distributions can increase federal and state taxes, cause more Social Security to become taxable, and raise Medicare premiums through IRMAA—years before long-term care is needed.

If care does occur, large taxable withdrawals can stack on top of pension income, Social Security, and RMDs. The retiree may have saved the account for the correct emergency while saving it in one of the least tax-friendly forms for using it quickly.

Evaluate the after-tax amount available for care and compare it with other strategies, including dedicated reserves, insurance, hybrid benefits, Roth assets, home equity, and family resources.

Required Minimum Does Not Mean Recommended Maximum

Traditional retirement accounts cannot remain tax-deferred forever. Required minimum distributions generally begin at an applicable statutory age.

Under current law, the starting age is generally seventy-three for people born from 1951 through 1959 and seventy-five for people born in 1960 or later. Older retirees can be governed by earlier starting ages. Roth TSP balances are no longer subject to lifetime RMDs for the original participant.

The RMD is calculated from the prior year-end balance and an IRS life-expectancy factor. It is the minimum amount that must come out—not an endorsement of the account's tax efficiency.

Waiting until RMD age may result in a larger balance and larger forced distributions. The retiree has successfully postponed taxes into the years when the government begins choosing the withdrawal schedule.

The First RMD Can Create a Two-RMD Year

A first RMD can generally be delayed until April 1 of the year following the year in which the applicable age is reached. Later RMDs are due by December 31.

Delaying the first distribution can place the first and second RMDs in the same tax year. That may increase taxable income, move the retiree into a higher bracket, and create additional IRMAA two years later.

Deferral can still make sense in a particular case. It should be modeled rather than accepted as free extra time.

Deadlines are not strategies. They are the last dates the government allows before becoming more personally involved.

The Retirement Tax Window

Many retirees experience a period after the final paycheck and before Social Security or RMDs begin. Taxable income may be lower during these years than it was while working or will be later in retirement.

That period is a tax window. It may provide room for Roth conversions, planned traditional TSP withdrawals, capital-gain realization, or other strategies at controlled rates.

The goal is not always to minimize this year's tax. A retiree may intentionally pay more tax now to reduce RMDs, improve future tax flexibility, lower survivor exposure, and leave more favorable assets to beneficiaries.

A zero-tax year can be a missed opportunity if it leaves a much larger account to be taxed later at higher effective rates.

Roth Conversions Are a Rate Decision

A Roth conversion moves pretax retirement money into a Roth account and generally includes the converted amount in taxable income for the year.

The conversion is attractive when the tax rate paid today is expected to be lower than the rate avoided later, after considering the retiree, spouse, beneficiaries, and Medicare effects. It is unattractive when someone converts merely because Roth sounds reassuring.

The TSP now permits eligible in-plan Roth conversions. A direct rollover to an IRA can also be followed by a Roth conversion under applicable rules. Each route has operational, withholding, investment, and planning differences.

Conversions are usually strongest when taxes can be paid from outside funds. Using retirement money for the tax reduces the amount reaching the Roth and may create additional consequences for someone under age fifty-nine and one-half.

Fill Brackets—Do Not Trip Over Cliffs

Tax brackets apply progressively. Moving into a higher bracket does not cause every dollar of income to be taxed at the higher rate. Only the dollars within that bracket receive the higher marginal rate.

IRMAA works differently. Medicare uses income tiers, and crossing a threshold can increase Part B and Part D costs for the year. Other deductions, credits, capital-gain rates, and Social Security taxation can create additional interactions.

A conversion that appears attractive using only the federal bracket may become less attractive after adding state tax and Medicare premiums. Another conversion may still be worthwhile despite IRMAA because the long-term RMD and survivor savings are larger.

The correct question is not, 'Will this trigger IRMAA?' It is, 'What is the total lifetime cost with and without the strategy?'

Auntie IRMAA Has a Two-Year Memory

Medicare generally uses modified adjusted gross income from two years earlier to determine IRMAA. A large conversion at age sixty-three can therefore affect premiums at sixty-five.

The additional amount applies separately to each Medicare beneficiary. A married couple can therefore feel one income event twice.

Because IRMAA thresholds and premiums change, projections should use current rules as estimates and preserve a margin for investment income, capital-gain distributions, and other surprises.

IRMAA is a cost, not a moral judgment. Sometimes it should be avoided. Sometimes it is the admission price for a strategy that saves substantially more elsewhere.

Social Security Has Its Own Tax Torpedo

Depending on provisional income, up to eighty-five percent of Social Security benefits can be included in federal taxable income. That does not mean the benefit is taxed at eighty-five percent. It means up to eighty-five percent becomes part of taxable income.

A TSP withdrawal can therefore create more taxable income than the distribution alone suggests because it can cause additional Social Security benefits to become taxable.

This interaction creates a higher effective marginal rate across certain income ranges. The retiree withdraws one dollar, but the tax return may add more than one dollar of taxable income.

Coordinating conversions and withdrawals before Social Security begins can reduce this problem, although the best claiming strategy must still consider longevity and survivor benefits.

The Survivor's Tax Problem

After the first spouse dies, household income often falls less than taxes expect. One Social Security check disappears, but the survivor may retain the larger benefit, a survivor pension, investment income, and future RMDs.

The survivor generally moves from married-filing-jointly brackets to single brackets. Standard deductions, tax thresholds, and IRMAA tiers can become less generous while many expenses remain.

This is the widow's or widower's tax problem. A strategy that appears acceptable while both spouses are alive can become expensive for the survivor.

Roth conversions, beneficiary design, survivor elections, Social Security staging, and account ownership should be evaluated through the survivor's future return—not only today's joint return.

Pretax Money Can Be a Difficult Inheritance

For many nonspouse beneficiaries, inherited retirement accounts must be emptied by the end of the tenth year after death. Depending on the owner's age and beneficiary category, annual distributions may also be required during the ten-year period.

The beneficiary generally pays ordinary income tax on inherited pretax distributions. The account may arrive during peak earning years, when the child is paying a mortgage, funding college, and already occupying a higher tax bracket.

Unlike many taxable investments, pretax retirement money does not receive a step-up that erases the embedded ordinary-income tax obligation. The beneficiary inherits both the asset and the tax problem attached to it.

Exceptions and special rules apply to spouses, minor children of the owner, disabled or chronically ill beneficiaries, and certain beneficiaries close in age to the owner. Estate and trust beneficiaries require additional care.

Legacy Planning Is About After-Tax Value

A beneficiary statement showing $500,000 does not tell the family how much legacy was created. The useful number is what remains after taxes, distribution deadlines, fees, and the beneficiary's circumstances.

Roth accounts can provide more favorable inherited income-tax treatment, though beneficiary distribution rules still apply. Taxable assets may receive a basis adjustment under current law. Life insurance death benefits are generally income-tax-free to beneficiaries when structured properly. Each asset has a different tax character and purpose.

The best asset to spend in retirement may be the worst asset to leave, and the best asset to leave may be inefficient for current spending.

Legacy planning should decide which assets go to which people and charities—not simply divide every account equally because the percentages were easy to type.

Charitable Giving Can Change the Tax Map

Charitably inclined retirees may have opportunities to direct retirement assets more efficiently.

A qualified charitable distribution can generally be made directly from an IRA—not directly from the TSP—once the taxpayer reaches the applicable QCD age. A QCD can satisfy eligible IRA RMD amounts while keeping the qualified distribution out of adjusted gross income, subject to annual limits and requirements.

A retiree may roll eligible TSP money to an IRA to facilitate future QCDs, but early-access rules, investment costs, creditor protection, and other planning factors must be considered before moving the account.

Naming charity as beneficiary of pretax retirement money can also be efficient because the charity generally does not pay income tax, while family may receive assets with more favorable tax treatment.

State Taxes Do Not Retire With You

States treat federal pensions, Social Security, TSP distributions, military benefits, and retirement income differently. Some provide exclusions; some tax most income; some have no individual income tax.

A move can change income taxes, property taxes, sales taxes, insurance costs, estate rules, and the price of healthcare and housing. Selecting a state because one tax rate is zero can be a costly way to discover the other columns in the budget.

Residency must be real. Keeping a house, driver's license, voter registration, business connection, or substantial time in a former state can create questions about domicile.

Choose where to live because it supports the life you want. Then understand the full financial result.

Withholding Is Not the Tax Bill

OPM, Social Security, the TSP, and IRA custodians may withhold taxes from payments. Withholding is a prepayment —not the final calculation.

Too little can create an unexpected balance and possible penalty. Too much gives the government an interest-free loan and reduces monthly cash flow.

Coordinate Form W-4P, W-4R, voluntary Social Security withholding, estimated payments, and other sources so the household pays reasonably throughout the year.

A large refund can feel pleasant. So can finding twenty dollars in an old coat. Neither proves the underlying plan was efficient.

Judge Hand and the Duty to Act

Judge Learned Hand famously wrote, 'There is not even a patriotic duty to increase one's taxes.' The point was not that taxes should be evaded. They should not. The point was that taxpayers may arrange their affairs within the law rather than volunteer the most expensive result.

Information alone does not arrange anything.

Knowing that RMDs may be large, IRMAA may apply, a survivor may face higher rates, and children may inherit a ten-year tax problem does not improve the outcome. Decisions made before year-end do.

If the retirement vision matters, the tax plan must move from education to implementation.

Your Purpose Driven Federal Employee Action Step

Build a Lifetime Federal Tax Map—not merely a projection for this April.

Income timeline Project pension, supplement, Social Security, TSP withdrawals, RMDs, investment income, and survivor income by year.

Tax buckets List traditional, Roth, and taxable balances and estimate their after-tax value.

Retirement window Identify the years between retirement and Social Security or RMDs when taxable income may be unusually low.

Conversion range Model partial Roth conversions across several years, including state tax and Medicare IRMAA.

RMD forecast Estimate future required distributions under current law rather than waiting for the first notice.

Complete the Survivor and Legacy Review

Survivor return Recalculate the plan using single tax brackets, one Social Security benefit, survivor pension income, and inherited accounts.

Long-term care Compare the after-tax TSP reserve with other ways to fund or insure the risk.

Beneficiary taxes Estimate when heirs must withdraw inherited pretax money and the rates they may pay.

Charitable strategy Determine whether QCDs or charitable beneficiary designations can redirect pretax dollars more efficiently.

Annual action Before December 31, decide what should be withdrawn, converted, realized, gifted, or withheld this year.

The goal is not the smallest tax bill in one isolated year. It is the greatest after-tax flexibility for your life, your surviving spouse, and the people and purposes you want your money to serve.

Chapter 9

Protect the People Who Retire With You

Retirement planning is often presented as a finish line for one person: your service, your pension, your TSP, your retirement date. But a household does not retire on an individual statement. It retires on an interconnected system of income, health coverage, taxes, insurance, and promises.

That system changes after the first death. One Social Security benefit may disappear. A pension may shrink. The tax return may change from married filing jointly to single. Medicare premiums may be measured against less generous thresholds. Meanwhile, the mortgage, property taxes, groceries, utilities, and the dog's firmly held opinions about premium treats do not become half-price.

A survivor plan is not a prediction about who dies first. It is an agreement that neither person should have to learn the federal benefit system while grieving.

The goal of this chapter is simple: make sure the people who retire with you remain protected when the plan must continue without you.

The First-Death Plan

A retirement income plan answers, 'Can we afford to retire?' A first-death plan asks, 'Can either one of us afford to stay retired?' Those are different calculations.

Run the plan twice—once with the employee dying first and once with the spouse dying first. The results may be very different. The employee's death can affect the federal pension,

FEHB eligibility, FEGLI, and TSP ownership. The spouse's death can remove Social Security, earnings, insurance, caregiving, or another pension.

For each scenario, list the income that stops, the income that continues, the assets that transfer, and the expenses that change. Then model taxes under the survivor's likely filing status.

'My spouse will be fine' is a loving sentiment. It is not yet a calculation.

Your Survivor Election Is an Insurance Decision

At retirement, a married federal employee generally chooses how much survivor annuity protection to provide. That election reduces the retiree's monthly annuity while both spouses are alive in exchange for income that may continue to the surviving spouse after the retiree's death.

It is tempting to judge the election only by asking how many years the survivor must live to recover the reductions. That treats the decision like an investment. It is better understood as insurance against the financial damage caused by an early death and the loss of lifetime income and health-benefit eligibility.

Insurance is rarely purchased because we hope to earn a handsome return from catastrophe. It is purchased because the household cannot comfortably absorb the loss.

The correct election depends on the survivor's income needs, age, health, longevity, assets, insurance, taxes, and FEHB. Selecting the smallest reduction on the retirement application without modeling those variables is not thrift. It is paperwork making a financial decision while you watch.

FERS Survivor Annuity Choices

Under FERS, the full survivor election generally provides an eligible spouse with fifty percent of the retiree's unreduced annuity. The retiree's annuity is generally reduced by ten percent to provide that protection.

A partial election generally provides twenty-five percent of the unreduced annuity and reduces the retiree's annuity by five percent. A married retiree generally needs the spouse's written consent to elect less than the maximum survivor benefit.

Suppose the unreduced FERS annuity is $48,000 per year. A full election would generally reduce the retiree's benefit by $4,800 per year and provide a survivor annuity of $24,000 per year. A partial election would generally reduce it by $2,400 and provide $12,000. This simplified example does not include taxes, COLAs, or special circumstances.

Notice what the decision is really doing. It is trading household income while both spouses are alive for protected income after one spouse dies. Whether that trade is appropriate cannot be determined from the reduction alone.

CSRS Uses Different Math

CSRS survivor elections follow different rules. A maximum CSRS survivor annuity is generally fifty-five percent of the retiree's unreduced annuity.

The reduction to provide a maximum benefit is generally two and one-half percent of the first $3,600 of the elected base plus ten percent of the amount above $3,600. A retiree may be able to select a smaller survivor base, subject to spousal-consent requirements.

Because the CSRS formula uses an elected base, comparisons should be performed with the actual annuity and survivor amounts—not a FERS rule remembered from a coworker's retirement seminar.

Federal benefits reward precision. They are less enthusiastic about folklore.

FEHB Makes the Election Bigger Than the Pension

For many married federal retirees, the survivor annuity election is also the gatekeeper for the surviving spouse's continued FEHB coverage.

In general, the spouse must be covered as a family member under the retiree's FEHB enrollment when the retiree dies and must be entitled to a survivor annuity. If there is no survivor annuity, continued FEHB coverage generally ends after the temporary extension of coverage.

A partial survivor election may preserve FEHB eligibility when the other requirements are met, but the survivor annuity must be large enough to support premium withholding or the survivor must arrange direct payment. The exact record should be verified before retirement.

This is why replacing a survivor annuity with life insurance is not a simple dollar-for-dollar exercise. A death benefit may replace income. It does not automatically replace the right to remain in FEHB.

Do Not Solve a Lifetime Problem With a Lump Sum Alone

A lump-sum life-insurance benefit can be valuable. It can pay debt, create liquidity, replace an income stream, fund care, or preserve a legacy. But the check arrives only once.

The survivor annuity is different. It provides monthly income for an eligible survivor's lifetime and may carry cost-of-living adjustments under applicable rules. It also may preserve FEHB eligibility.

When comparing the two, model how much capital would be required to reproduce the survivor annuity through an uncertain lifetime, including investment risk, inflation, taxes, fees, and the survivor's willingness to manage money.

Sometimes insurance and other assets can support a reduced survivor election. Sometimes the full election is clearly stronger. The answer belongs to the household's complete plan, not to a slogan about pensions or insurance.

Marriage, Divorce, and Timing Rules

Survivor benefits can change with marriage, remarriage, divorce, and court orders. Those events should trigger an immediate federal-benefits review—not a note to handle it eventually.

A FERS retiree who marries after retirement and did not already provide the applicable survivor protection generally must notify OPM within two years of the marriage to elect a benefit for the new spouse. The election can require both the regular annuity reduction and an actuarial deposit, with interest, for prior payments.

A qualifying court order can award survivor benefits to a former spouse and limit what remains available for a current spouse. A divorce decree, beneficiary form, and OPM record can each affect a different benefit.

Have an attorney experienced in federal retirement orders review the language before the divorce is final. 'We will divide the pension fairly' may sound agreeable in mediation and become a small archaeological expedition at OPM.

Social Security Becomes a One-Check Household

When both spouses receive Social Security and one dies, the survivor generally does not keep both full checks. The survivor typically receives the benefit for which they qualify under survivor rules—often the larger of the two amounts—not the sum of both benefits.

That makes the higher earner's claiming decision a survivor decision as well as an individual break-even decision. Delaying the higher earner's benefit can increase the income that may remain for the survivor.

The household may lose one check while retaining much of the same housing, transportation, and healthcare spending. Taxes can also become less forgiving after the survivor begins filing as a single taxpayer.

Model Social Security alongside the federal survivor annuity. Two individually reasonable elections can combine into a household shortfall if no one adds them together.

FEGLI Is a Benefit—Not a Strategy by Itself

Federal Employees' Group Life Insurance is group term insurance. It can be convenient, requires no medical underwriting during certain enrollment opportunities, and may be carried into retirement when eligibility rules are satisfied.

To continue FEGLI into retirement, an employee generally must retire on an immediate annuity and have been enrolled in the coverage for the five years immediately before retirement—or for all service since the first opportunity to enroll if that period is shorter.

FEGLI has no cash value. Coverage and premiums can change according to the option, age, and reduction election. That does not make it good or bad. It means the policy needs a defined job.

The useful question is not, 'Should I keep FEGLI?' It is, 'What financial loss must life insurance cover, for how long, and which contract does that job most efficiently?'

Basic FEGLI After Retirement

Basic FEGLI is based on the employee's Basic Insurance Amount, generally annual basic pay rounded up to the next $1,000 plus $2,000. At retirement, an eligible participant chooses a seventy-five-percent reduction, fifty-percent reduction, or no reduction.

With the seventy-five-percent reduction, Basic coverage begins reducing after age sixty-five or retirement, whichever is later. It generally falls by two percent of the preretirement amount each month until twenty-five percent remains. The retiree no longer pays a Basic premium once reductions begin.

With the fifty-percent reduction, coverage generally falls by one percent per month until fifty percent remains, and an additional premium continues. With no reduction, the full amount remains, but the retiree pays an additional premium that can become substantial with age.

A reduction can be entirely appropriate when insurance needs fall as assets grow and debts decline. No reduction may be appropriate when a permanent death-benefit need remains. The election should follow the job—not nostalgia for the benefit statement.

Options A, B, and C Have Their Own Rules

Option A provides $10,000 of additional coverage. In retirement, eligible Option A coverage generally reduces automatically by two percent per month until $2,500 remains, with premiums ending when the reduction begins.

Option B provides additional coverage in multiples of annual basic pay. At retirement, the participant chooses how many multiples will fully reduce and how many will continue without reduction. Fully reducing multiples generally decline two percent per month for fifty months until they reach zero. No-reduction multiples remain in force with age-based premiums.

Option C covers eligible family members in one to five multiples. Each multiple represents a stated amount for a spouse and a smaller amount for each eligible child. Retirees choose which multiples fully reduce to zero and which continue without reduction, subject to the program's rules and premiums.

Option B and C premiums can rise sharply in later age bands. Keeping coverage because it has always been there is not analysis. Review the current rate chart and the benefit that will actually remain.

FEGLI Is Not the Only Kind of Life Insurance

Term insurance is designed to provide a death benefit for a stated period or while premiums remain affordable. Permanent insurance may provide lifetime coverage, cash value, guarantees, or other features when properly funded and maintained.

Some modern policies can include chronic-illness or long-term-care benefits. Others may support legacy, estate-liquidity, charitable, or survivor-income goals. These features come with costs, underwriting, contract limitations, and carrier risk that must be understood.

The point is not that private insurance is automatically better than FEGLI—or that permanent insurance is automatically better than term. There are many types of insurance because there are many types of financial problems.

Compare guarantees, premiums, reduction schedules, underwriting, flexibility, policy charges, and the consequences of changing course. A trained adviser should explain both what a contract does and what it does not do.

Give Every Death Benefit a Job

Life insurance is easier to evaluate when every dollar has an assignment. One portion may replace the pension or Social Security that disappears. Another may pay off a mortgage. Another may create a long-term-care reserve, equalize inheritances, support a child, or fund a charitable gift.

Estimate the amount and duration of each need. A ten-year income bridge is different from a lifetime legacy. A mortgage payoff is different from FEHB premiums. A special-needs beneficiary may require trust planning rather than a direct payment.

Then match the benefit to the need. Temporary risks may fit term coverage. Permanent needs may require assets, survivor income, permanent coverage, or a combination.

Insurance without a job becomes a premium. Insurance with a job becomes part of the plan.

Beneficiary Forms Can Overrule Family Intentions

Federal benefits do not automatically follow the will. FEGLI, the TSP, unpaid compensation, and retirement contributions each have their own beneficiary rules, forms, and orders of precedence.

A valid FEGLI designation must be received by the proper office before death. The TSP maintains its own beneficiary designation process. If no valid designation exists, benefits are generally paid under the program's statutory order—not according to a conversation at the kitchen table.

Common federal forms include SF 2823 for FEGLI, SF 3102 for FERS retirement contributions, SF 2808 for CSRS retirement contributions, and SF 1152 for unpaid compensation. TSP designations are maintained through the participant's TSP account under current procedures.

Forms and procedures change. Verify the current method, confirm receipt, keep evidence, and review the actual record —not the unsigned copy discovered in a desk drawer.

The Beneficiary Audit

Review beneficiary records after marriage, divorce, birth, adoption, death, estrangement, a trust change, or a major financial event. Also review them periodically when nothing dramatic has happened, because memory is not a records-management system.

Check primary and contingent beneficiaries, percentages, legal names, dates of birth, addresses, and whether any beneficiary is a minor. Confirm that the designation coordinates with the will, trusts, account ownership, and the intended tax result.

A spouse and a nonspouse beneficiary can face different TSP options and tax rules. A trust or estate designation can produce results very different from naming an individual. Special-needs beneficiaries require particular care to avoid disrupting public benefits.

Use a qualified estate-planning attorney for trusts, minors, special needs, blended families, creditor concerns, or complex estates. A beneficiary form is short. Its consequences may last for decades.

Your TSP Needs a Successor Plan

The TSP beneficiary designation decides who receives the account. The successor plan decides what that person should do next.

A surviving spouse generally has options that differ from those available to a nonspouse beneficiary. Nonspouse beneficiaries can face inherited-account distribution deadlines and ordinary-income tax on pretax money. Leaving a large traditional TSP may therefore transfer both wealth and a compressed tax problem.

Coordinate the beneficiary designation with Roth-conversion planning, life insurance, charitable goals, and the beneficiary's likely tax bracket. Equal percentages do not always create equal after-tax inheritances.

Leave instructions to seek tax advice before moving or withdrawing the account. Grief is an expensive time to discover that a helpful relative has strong opinions about rollovers and no professional liability insurance.

Build the 'If Something Happens' File

The best survivor plan can fail if no one can find it. Create a secure physical or digital file that tells the survivor what exists, whom to call, and what must happen first.

Include current OPM retirement records, FEHB and Medicare information, FEGLI coverage, TSP and other account lists, beneficiary confirmations, insurance policies, Social Security information, tax returns, estate documents, debts, recurring bills, and professional contacts.

Do not place unprotected passwords in an ordinary binder. Instead, document where secure credentials and multifactor-recovery instructions are maintained. Include instructions for obtaining death certificates and notifying OPM, Social Security, the TSP, insurers, and financial institutions.

Review the file together. A beautifully organized binder known only to the person who died is less of a plan and more of a final scavenger hunt.

Specialized Advice Matters Here

Federal survivor planning crosses several professional lanes: retirement rules, FEHB, life insurance, investments, income taxes, Social Security, and estate law. One recommendation can affect all of them.

A financial professional with the Chartered Federal Employee Benefits Consultant℠ (ChFEBC℠) designation has received specialized training in federal employee benefits. The designation does not replace tax or legal counsel, and no credential eliminates the need to verify current rules. It does help identify a planner who has studied the federal system rather than meeting it for the first time inside your retirement application.

The strongest team may include a ChFEBC-trained financial professional, CPA or enrolled agent, estate-planning attorney, and—when needed—an attorney experienced with federal retirement or divorce orders.

Coordination is the service. A perfect answer in one silo can create an expensive mistake in another.

Information Must Become Protection

You can understand every survivor option and still leave your spouse exposed. Knowledge does not create a survivor annuity, update a beneficiary, fund an insurance policy, or show someone where the documents are kept.

The federal benefit system will generally follow the election, designation, court order, and record in force—not what the family remembers you intended.

This chapter is not asking you to become an expert in every rule. It is asking you to take responsibility for the decisions that cannot be repaired after death.

If the retirement vision includes the people you love, protecting their version of that life is part of the plan—not an appendix to it.

Your Purpose Driven Federal Employee Action Step

Build the First-Death Plan. Complete it for both possible orders of death.

Survivor income Calculate the FERS or CSRS survivor annuity, remaining Social Security, other pensions, insurance proceeds, and sustainable portfolio income.

FEHB continuity Confirm that the survivor election and enrollment records preserve the intended spouse's eligibility and that premiums can be paid.

Household expenses Identify which costs disappear, which remain, and which may rise because one person must purchase help previously provided by the other.

Tax return Project the survivor's income using single tax brackets, one Social Security benefit, RMDs, and applicable IRMAA thresholds.

FEGLI review List Basic, Option A, Option B, and Option C coverage; the retirement reduction election; future premiums; and the purpose of each benefit.

Complete the Insurance and Beneficiary Review

Insurance comparison Compare FEGLI with other term, permanent, hybrid, or asset-based solutions using guarantees, costs, underwriting, and the job to be done.

Beneficiary audit Verify current FEGLI, TSP, retirement-contribution, unpaid-compensation, IRA, insurance, and other account designations.

Estate coordination Confirm that beneficiary forms, wills, trusts, titles, powers of attorney, and healthcare documents tell one coherent story.

Successor instructions Document whom the survivor should call before making TSP, tax, insurance, or rollover decisions.

Emergency file Create the secure 'if something happens' file and review its location and contents together.

The measure of a survivor plan is not how complete it looks while both spouses are alive. It is whether the person left behind has enough income, continued healthcare, clear instructions, and the freedom to grieve without immediately becoming a federal-benefits specialist.

Chapter 10

Long-Term Care—Protecting More Than Your TSP

Long-term care is one of those subjects people prefer to schedule for later—ideally on the thirty-second of Never. Nobody wants to imagine needing help bathing, dressing, eating, moving safely, managing medications, or recognizing the people they love.

Avoiding the subject does not remove the risk. It merely reserves the decision for a future version of the family who may have fewer choices, less time, and much more stress.

For federal employees, the conversation often begins with a reassuring collection of initials: FEHB, Medicare, FLTCIP, TSP. Unfortunately, initials do not coordinate themselves. Health insurance is not the same as custodial-care coverage, the federal long-term-care program may not be open to new applicants, and a large traditional TSP can create taxes precisely when the family needs liquidity.

Long-term-care planning protects more than money. It protects the healthy spouse, the children, the caregiver, the home, the family's time, and the retiree's dignity and choices.

Begin With the Care—not the Product

The first question is not, 'Which policy should I buy?' It is, 'If I need care, what do I want that care to look like?'

Would you prefer to remain at home? Live near children? Move to an assisted-living or continuing-care community?

Who do you imagine will help? Does that person live nearby, have a job, raise children, manage health concerns, or know they have been cast in this role?

A person may begin with a few hours of weekly help, progress to daily assistance, and eventually require constant supervision. Care can occur at home, through adult day services, in assisted living, in memory care, or in a nursing facility. The setting, duration, and intensity determine much of the cost.

Design the care plan first. Financing should support the life and choices you want—not force the family into whichever option happens to be affordable during a crisis.

Long-Term Care Is Not Just a Nursing Home

Most long-term care is help with ordinary activities of daily living or supervision caused by cognitive impairment. It may involve bathing, dressing, eating, toileting, continence, transferring, medication management, meal preparation, transportation, or safety.

Some care is medical and skilled. Much of it is personal or custodial. That distinction matters because the program paying the hospital bill may not pay someone to help a parent get dressed every morning.

Care needs can rise gradually. A spouse may help at first, then the household hires an aide, modifies the home, adds transportation, and eventually considers a community with greater support.

A good plan anticipates a spectrum rather than betting everything on one facility, one child, or one cost estimate.

FEHB Is Excellent Health Coverage—not Long-Term-Care Insurance

FEHB—and PSHB for eligible Postal Service employees and annuitants—can provide valuable medical coverage throughout retirement when continuation rules are satisfied. It can pay for covered physicians, hospitals, prescriptions, therapies, and other medical services according to the plan.

It is not designed to pay indefinitely for assistance with daily living when custodial care is the primary need. A health plan may cover certain skilled or medically necessary services without covering years of home aides, assisted living, or nursing-home custodial care.

Review the actual plan brochure for covered skilled-nursing, home-health, rehabilitation, hospice, and related benefits. Do not translate a limited medical benefit into an unlimited care promise.

FEHB is a powerful retirement asset. Asking it to become long-term-care insurance is simply giving a very good benefit the wrong job.

Medicare Does Not Become the Missing Policy

Medicare may cover qualifying skilled-nursing-facility or home-health services for a limited period when its conditions are met. It generally does not cover long-term custodial care when that is the only care needed.

The famous 'one hundred days' is not a guaranteed one-hundred-day nursing-home benefit. Skilled-nursing coverage depends on eligibility, continued need for covered skilled care, benefit-period rules, and cost sharing. Custodial residence is different.

Medicare Advantage plans can have different networks, authorization requirements, and cost sharing, but they do not transform Medicare into comprehensive long-term-care insurance. Medigap helps with certain Medicare cost sharing; it does not create coverage for services Medicare excludes.

Keep Medicare and FEHB for medical care. Build a separate strategy for extended personal care.

The Federal Long Term Care Insurance Program

The Federal Long Term Care Insurance Program, commonly called FLTCIP, was created for eligible federal and Postal employees, annuitants, members of the uniformed services, and certain qualified relatives. The enrollee—not the employing agency—generally pays the full premium.

As this book is being prepared, OPM has suspended new applications and increases in coverage for current enrollees. Existing coverage has not simply vanished, but someone who is not enrolled cannot assume the federal program is available. The suspension has been extended before, so readers should verify the current status directly with OPM and LTCFEDS.

The suspension is an important planning lesson: an employee benefit is not a strategy until you know you are eligible, the program is available, underwriting is satisfied, and the contract fits the need.

Do not wait until retirement to investigate the risk. Health can change, private coverage may require underwriting, and the marketplace may offer fewer choices later.

If You Already Own FLTCIP

Current FLTCIP policyholders should review the policy rather than placing the statement in the same drawer as the passport and assuming the matter is complete.

Identify the daily benefit amount, benefit period, waiting period, inflation feature, covered settings, benefit triggers, premium, and total pool of money. Determine whether the coverage is shared or individual and what happens when benefits begin.

Long-term-care insurance premiums and benefit structures can change subject to the policy and regulatory approvals. If a premium increase creates concern, evaluate available options and the effect of reducing or surrendering coverage before acting. Replacement may require new underwriting and may not be available.

A policy bought years ago may be highly valuable, insufficient by itself, or one layer of a broader plan. The only way to know is to compare its future benefit with the care you want and the resources you will have.

Four Ways to Fund the Risk

Most long-term-care plans use one or more of four broad resources: personal assets, traditional long-term-care insurance, hybrid insurance, and public or veterans' programs for those who qualify.

Self-funding means using income, savings, investments, retirement accounts, or home equity. Traditional coverage is designed specifically to reimburse or pay benefits for qualifying care under the contract. Hybrid strategies combine life insurance or an annuity with long-term-care or chronic-illness features. Public programs operate under eligibility and coverage rules that can differ by state and change over time.

There is no universal winner. Each approach trades premiums, liquidity, guarantees, underwriting, opportunity cost, tax treatment, benefit limits, and legacy value.

The best answer may be a combination: retain enough assets for the first portion of a care event while transferring the risk that would threaten the healthy spouse or the family's essential goals.

Self-Funding Means You Are the Insurance Company

'We will self-fund' can be an entirely reasonable conclusion. It should not be a polished way of saying, 'We have not looked at it.'

A real self-funding plan identifies the assets, their after-tax value, the expected sequence of use, the effect on income, and the amount that must remain for the healthy spouse. It also tests a longer or more expensive event than the family hopes to experience.

Ask what happens if one spouse needs several years of care. Must investments be sold during a market decline? Does the survivor lose income? Is the house sold? Does the portfolio become too depleted or too conservative? What happens if both spouses eventually need help?

If the balance sheet can absorb those outcomes without sacrificing essential goals, self-funding may be strong. If not, the household is not self-insured. It is uninsured with confidence.

The Traditional TSP Is a Gross Care Reserve

Many federal retirees say, 'We are saving the TSP for long-term care.' The intention is responsible. The tax structure may be less cooperative.

Traditional TSP withdrawals generally create ordinary taxable income. A large withdrawal for care can stack on top of pension income, Social Security, investment income, and required minimum distributions. It can also increase future Medicare IRMAA because Medicare generally looks back two years at modified adjusted gross income.

Some qualified long-term-care expenses may produce medical deductions when tax requirements are met, but deductions depend on adjusted gross income, itemizing, timing, and the nature of the expense. Do not assume a large care withdrawal will be neatly canceled by a deduction.

Measure the care reserve after tax. Then consider whether planned withdrawals, Roth conversions, insurance, taxable assets, or other resources can create more flexible dollars before the crisis arrives.

Traditional Long-Term-Care Insurance

Traditional long-term-care insurance can transfer part of the financial risk in exchange for premiums. Policies may cover qualifying home care, adult day care, assisted living, memory care, nursing facilities, or other services depending on the contract.

Compare the monthly benefit, benefit period or pool, elimination period, inflation protection, benefit triggers, reimbursement versus indemnity design, care coordination, exclusions, premium history, and insurer strength.

The benefit usually begins only after the insured meets the contract's eligibility requirements, commonly involving inability to perform specified activities of daily living or severe cognitive impairment, and after any elimination-period conditions are satisfied.

The criticism that someone may pay premiums and never collect a claim is mathematically true and philosophically incomplete. That is how insurance works when the event you insured against does not happen. The real question is whether transferring the risk improves the plan.

Hybrid Life and Long-Term-Care Strategies

Some life-insurance contracts include long-term-care riders or chronic-illness features. Other products are designed specifically to combine a death benefit with a pool for qualifying care. Certain annuity-based designs can also provide enhanced benefits for care.

These strategies may appeal to someone who wants value available whether care is needed or not. If qualifying care occurs, benefits may be accessed under the contract. If they are not fully used, a death benefit or account value may remain.

Hybrid does not mean magical. Contracts differ in benefit triggers, reimbursement methods, residual death benefits, inflation options, premiums, liquidity, surrender values, tax treatment, and guarantees. Chronic-illness and qualified long-term-care riders are not interchangeable labels.

Start with the risk. Then determine whether the contract solves it efficiently. A product demonstration should never be allowed to invent the problem after the illustration is printed.

Protect the Healthy Spouse

The most important long-term-care question may not be, 'How will we pay for care?' It may be, 'How will we pay for care without destroying the healthy spouse's retirement?'

The spouse who does not need care still needs housing, food, transportation, medical coverage, income, and a future. The household may also lose income when the spouse receiving care dies, making Chapter 9's survivor plan part of this calculation.

Separate essential survivor capital from the assets available for care. Test the survivor pension, Social Security, taxes, TSP balance, insurance, and housing costs after a long care event—not just before it.

A plan that pays every care bill but leaves the healthy spouse financially insecure has solved only half the problem.

Home Care Requires Infrastructure

Most people say they want to remain at home. Home is familiar, personal, and filled with memories. It may also have three flights of stairs, narrow doors, a slippery tub, no nearby caregivers, and a driveway that becomes its own winter sport.

Aging in place may require aides, nurses, transportation, meals, housekeeping, home modifications, safety equipment, monitoring technology, backup power, and someone to coordinate it all. Round-the-clock home care can require several caregivers and substantial cost.

Evaluate whether the home can support one-level living, accessible bathing, safe entrances, mobility equipment, and proximity to healthcare and family. Consider maintenance, taxes, insurance, and the ability of a surviving spouse to manage the property.

Aging in place is not simply declining to move. It is building a home, care network, and budget capable of keeping you there safely.

The Community Decision

Independent-living, assisted-living, continuing-care, and life-plan communities can provide social connection, meals, transportation, maintenance, and access to higher levels of care. The lifestyle may be as important as the healthcare promise.

Contracts can include entrance fees, monthly charges, refundable and nonrefundable provisions, financial qualification, healthcare guarantees, and different levels of included care. Two communities with similar brochures can create very different obligations.

Review the contract, fee history, financial condition, care availability, transfer rules, refund terms, and what happens if one spouse requires more care than the other. Use legal and financial professionals familiar with these agreements.

Tour the dining room and the balance sheet. Both can affect how much you enjoy living there.

Family Care Is Loving—but It Is Not Free

Family members provide extraordinary unpaid care. That care can be an expression of love and still carry a real cost.

A daughter may reduce work hours, decline a promotion, use leave, drive to appointments, manage medications, prepare meals, handle bills, and spend less time with her own household. A spouse may become physically exhausted or suffer health problems while providing care.

Those costs may never appear on the retiree's statement. They appear in lost earnings, reduced retirement savings, stress, injury, relationships, and time.

If a family member is part of the plan, discuss the role in advance. Decide whether compensation, backup care, respite, leave, or professional support will be available. Love should be invited into the plan—not drafted without notice.

Cognitive Decline Is Also a Financial Risk

A person can appear physically healthy while losing the ability to pay bills, evaluate investments, recognize scams, drive safely, manage medications, protect passwords, or understand contracts.

That is why durable powers of attorney, healthcare directives, trusted contacts, account alerts, document access, and a succession plan for financial management belong in the long-term-care strategy.

Consolidate unnecessary accounts and document recurring income and bills. Decide who can speak with OPM, the TSP, Social Security, insurers, banks, and healthcare providers when authorization is needed.

Complexity that feels intellectually stimulating at sixty-five can feel like an escape room to the eighty-five-year-old spouse trying to help.

Medicaid and Veterans' Benefits

Medicaid can pay for certain long-term services and supports for people who meet medical and financial eligibility requirements. Rules, covered settings, income limits, asset treatment, estate recovery, and spousal protections vary by state and circumstance.

Veterans and surviving spouses may qualify for certain care, pension, or Aid and Attendance-related benefits when service, financial, medical, and other requirements are met. Availability and eligibility should be confirmed with an appropriate accredited professional or agency.

Do not give away assets or retitle property based on a seminar promise. Transfers can affect eligibility, taxes, control, creditor exposure, and estate planning. Medicaid planning requires qualified elder-law counsel in the relevant state.

Public benefits can be an important layer. They should be evaluated as programs with rules—not treated as a vague promise that 'the government will take care of it.'

The ChFEBC-Coordinated Review

Federal employees need a plan that coordinates the care decision with the pension, survivor election, FEHB or PSHB, Medicare, TSP taxes, insurance, and beneficiary strategy.

A financial professional with the Chartered Federal Employee Benefits Consultant℠ (ChFEBC℠) designation has specialized training in federal employee benefits. That training can help connect federal programs to the broader retirement plan, while insurance, tax, legal, and care professionals address their respective areas.

No designation substitutes for reading the contract or verifying current program rules. FLTCIP availability, premiums, tax limits, Medicare costs, Medicaid rules, and private products can change.

The value is coordination: choosing which dollars pay first, which risks are transferred, what remains for the healthy spouse, and who will carry out the plan.

Have the Conversation While You Have Choices

Tell the people you love where you want care, who should make decisions, what resources and insurance exist, where the documents are stored, and what role you expect each person to play.

Do not make one child the entire plan by accident. One person might coordinate healthcare, another may help with finances, professionals may manage investments and legal work, and paid caregivers may provide daily support.

You do not need to disclose every account balance at the first family meeting. You do need to prevent the first family meeting from occurring in a hospital hallway while everyone's phone battery is at twelve percent.

Planning cannot guarantee perfect health or remove every burden. It can preserve choices, reduce conflict, protect the healthy spouse, and give the family a map when it needs one most.

Your Purpose Driven Federal Employee Action Step

Build a care plan, a financial plan, and a communication plan. Missing any one of the three makes the other two harder to use.

Care setting Write where you would prefer to receive care at each stage and what alternatives would be acceptable.

People Identify who you expect to help, discuss the role with them, and arrange professional and respite support.

Healthy spouse Calculate the income and capital that must remain protected if one spouse experiences an extended care event.

Current coverage Review FLTCIP or private policy benefits, triggers, inflation protection, elimination period, premiums, and covered settings.

Federal coverage Separate what FEHB or PSHB and Medicare cover from the custodial services they generally do not cover.

Complete the Funding and Family Review

Funding order Identify which income, taxable assets, Roth assets, traditional TSP dollars, insurance benefits, and home equity would be used—and in what order.

Tax impact Estimate taxes and possible future IRMAA from large traditional-account withdrawals and determine whether advance planning improves flexibility.

Housing Evaluate accessibility, transportation, maintenance, proximity to care, and the feasibility of aging in place.

Legal authority Confirm durable financial powers, healthcare directives, HIPAA permissions, trusts, and state-specific documents with qualified counsel.

Family meeting Explain the plan, responsibilities, professional contacts, document location, and what you do not expect children to provide.

The best long-term-care plan is not necessarily the policy with the largest benefit or the portfolio with the largest balance. It is the plan that gives you meaningful choices, protects the person who remains healthy, and allows your family to be your family—not an unpaid emergency response department.

Chapter 11

Estate Planning—When Federal Forms Meet Family Intentions

When people hear estate planning, they often picture a will, a solemn attorney's office, and a future event nobody has volunteered to place on the calendar. Federal employees need a wider picture.

A federal estate plan includes legal documents, but it also includes TSP beneficiary records, FEGLI designations, survivor elections, unpaid compensation, retirement contributions, account ownership, taxes, digital access, and the people who must make decisions if you cannot.

The will may be beautifully drafted and still have no authority over an asset controlled by a beneficiary designation or federal order of precedence. In other words, the document everyone calls 'my estate plan' may not control some of the household's largest assets.

Estate planning begins with a purpose question: What—and whom—do you want to take care of? The documents are tools. The people are the point.

What Do You Want the Money to Do?

'Everything goes equally to the children' may be a perfectly sound answer. It is still worth asking one level deeper: What do you want the inheritance to accomplish?

Perhaps you want to protect a spouse, educate grandchildren, support a church or charity, preserve family property, provide for a person with special needs, continue a business, or simply spare the family a financial mess.

Those goals may call for different assets, beneficiaries, timing, and legal structures. A traditional TSP account, Roth account, taxable investment, home, and life-insurance benefit may all show the same statement value while delivering very different after-tax results.

Begin with 'I want...' before completing 'I leave....' Purpose should write the assignment before paperwork chooses the route.

Estate Planning Is Retirement Planning

A complete retirement plan answers three questions: How do I care for myself while I am alive? How do I protect the people who depend on me? What happens to what remains?

The order matters. Giving away assets too early can weaken long-term-care security. Preserving every dollar for heirs can prevent the retiree from living the life the money was accumulated to support. Ignoring survivor income can leave a spouse asset-rich and cash-flow poor.

First protect your life and independence. Then protect the people who rely on you. Finally, direct what remains with intention.

Legacy is not the pile left untouched. It is every useful thing the money does along the way.

Your Will Does Not Control Every Federal Benefit

A will generally controls assets passing through probate under state law. Many federal benefits pass outside the will according to a designation, court order, program rule, or statutory order of precedence.

TSP accounts use the TSP's beneficiary process. FEGLI follows its designation and order rules. Lump-sum retirement contributions and unpaid compensation have their own records. A survivor annuity follows the retirement election and applicable law—not a paragraph added to the will later.

Joint ownership, transfer-on-death registrations, payable-on-death accounts, trusts, and insurance contracts can also direct property outside probate.

The will is essential for many households. It is not the chairman of every committee simply because it has the nicest binder.

The Federal Beneficiary Map

Create a one-page map showing every benefit, the current primary and contingent beneficiary, the controlling record, and the date it was verified.

Common federal records include the TSP beneficiary designation; SF 2823 for FEGLI; SF 3102 for FERS retirement contributions; SF 2808 for CSRS retirement contributions; and SF 1152 for unpaid compensation. Different rules apply to different payments, and forms or procedures may change.

A designation is not effective merely because a signed copy exists at home. For example, a FEGLI designation must be properly completed and received by the appropriate office before death. Confirm the correct filing destination and retain proof of receipt when available.

If you are satisfied with a program's statutory order of precedence, a designation may not be necessary. But that should be an intentional decision based on the current family —not the accidental result of never logging in.

TSP Beneficiaries Need More Than a Name

The TSP beneficiary designation determines who receives the account. The successor strategy determines what happens next.

A surviving spouse designated to receive TSP assets can generally receive a beneficiary participant account with special TSP treatment and options. A nonspouse beneficiary cannot retain a permanent TSP account; the TSP may establish a temporary account while the beneficiary selects an available payment or transfer option.

Those differences matter. A surviving spouse may have rollover and timing choices unavailable to children or other beneficiaries. A nonspouse beneficiary may be able to transfer eligible money to an inherited IRA rather than receiving a fully taxable check, but the transaction must be handled correctly and promptly.

Leave instructions to consult a qualified tax professional before moving the account. Bereavement is not improved by an avoidable five-figure tax surprise.

Pretax TSP Money Carries an Inherited Tax Bill

Traditional TSP money generally remains taxable as ordinary income when distributed to a beneficiary. For many nonspouse beneficiaries, current law requires the inherited retirement account to be emptied by the end of the tenth year after death. Depending on the owner's status and the beneficiary category, distributions may also be required during that period.

The inheritance may arrive during the child's peak earning years. A $500,000 traditional account is therefore not economically identical to $500,000 of Roth money, taxable investments with a potential basis adjustment, or properly structured life-insurance proceeds.

Eligible designated beneficiaries—including certain spouses, minor children of the owner, disabled or chronically ill individuals, and beneficiaries not more than ten years younger—can be subject to different rules. Trusts and estates introduce additional complexity.

Model the beneficiary's likely after-tax value. Estate planning that compares only statement balances can divide the numbers equally while dividing the benefit unequally.

Roth and Taxable Assets Have Different Jobs

Qualified Roth distributions can provide beneficiaries with more favorable income-tax treatment, though inherited-account distribution deadlines can still apply. Taxable investments may receive a basis adjustment at death under current law, while income in respect of a decedent—such as pretax retirement money—generally carries its embedded tax obligation forward.

That does not mean the retiree should preserve every Roth dollar and spend every taxable asset. The household still needs liquidity, income, tax control, and long-term-care resources.

It does mean lifetime Roth conversion planning, withdrawal sequencing, charitable designations, and beneficiary choices should be connected to the estate plan.

The best asset to spend may differ from the best asset to leave. The tax return, inconveniently, has opinions about sentiment.

FEGLI and Other Life Insurance

Life-insurance death benefits are generally received income-tax-free by beneficiaries when structured properly, making insurance a potentially efficient source of survivor liquidity, debt repayment, inheritance equalization, charitable support, or legacy.

FEGLI follows federal assignment, court-order, beneficiary, and order-of-precedence rules. A stale designation can defeat the family's current intentions. Coverage may also reduce in retirement depending on the election, so the amount listed years earlier may not be the amount paid at death.

Private life insurance has its own ownership and beneficiary provisions. Trust ownership can sometimes serve estate or control objectives but requires qualified legal and tax advice. Policy loans, assignments, ownership transfers, and incidents of ownership can affect results.

Review both the beneficiary and the benefit projected to remain. A perfectly named recipient of a benefit that has reduced to zero receives excellent paperwork and no money.

Survivor Benefits Are Not Beneficiary Accounts

A FERS or CSRS survivor annuity is governed by the retirement election, marital status, court orders, and federal law. It is not a lump-sum account that can be reassigned through the will.

The surviving spouse's FEHB eligibility can depend on being covered at death and entitled to an eligible survivor annuity. This makes the retirement election part of the estate plan even though no beneficiary statement displays an account balance.

A former spouse may hold rights under a qualifying court order. A later marriage can create deadlines and costs for electing coverage. The current spouse's expectations should be compared with the actual OPM record.

Chapter 9 built the first-death plan. Estate planning makes sure the legal documents and federal records do not quietly disagree with it.

Estate Planning Is Also About Incapacity

Some of the most important estate documents are used while you are alive. If illness, injury, or cognitive decline prevents you from acting, someone may need authority to manage finances, make healthcare decisions, access records, and communicate with institutions.

A durable financial power of attorney, advance medical directive, healthcare power, HIPAA authorization, living will, and trust provisions can serve different purposes under state law. Generic internet forms may not address the household, state, or federal institutions involved.

Confirm whether agents can handle retirement accounts, tax filings, insurance, real estate, digital property, government benefits, gifting, and trust matters as intended. Institutions may have additional procedures for recognizing authority.

Estate planning is not only about who receives property after death. It is also about who protects you before then.

Choose People for the Job

The person you love most is not automatically the best person for every fiduciary role. An executor, trustee, financial agent, healthcare decision-maker, guardian, and digital executor may require different judgment and skills.

The person may need to maintain records, follow legal duties, manage investments, coordinate professionals, communicate with family, and make decisions others dislike. Authority granted by a document cannot manufacture temperament.

Name successors in case the first person cannot serve. Discuss the responsibility in advance and make sure the person knows where to find the plan.

Surprising someone with the role of executor is the estate-planning equivalent of leaving a puppy on the porch—except the paperwork lasts longer.

Trusts: Start With the Problem

'Do I need a trust?' is not the first question. Ask what problem needs solving.

A trust may help manage assets during incapacity, avoid probate for properly titled assets, provide privacy, control distributions, protect young or vulnerable beneficiaries, address property in multiple states, support tax planning, or provide for a family member with special needs.

A trust does not control an asset that was never transferred to it or directed to it. Funding and beneficiary coordination are as important as signing the agreement.

Complexity carries legal fees, tax reporting, administration, and family confusion. Use a trust when it solves a meaningful problem—not because the binder looks more prosperous with one.

Special Needs Require Special Planning

Leaving assets directly to a person receiving means-tested public benefits can disrupt eligibility. Naming that person outright on TSP, FEGLI, or other beneficiary records may create the very problem the inheritance was intended to solve.

A properly designed special-needs or supplemental-needs trust may preserve resources for the beneficiary while coordinating with public benefits. The correct structure depends on who funds it, the beneficiary's circumstances, state law, and program requirements.

Work with an attorney experienced in special-needs planning and coordinate every beneficiary designation. The trust language and the federal form must point to the intended legal recipient correctly.

Care planning, successor trustees, advocates, housing, and a letter of intent can be as important as the dollars.

Equal and Fair Are Not Always Identical

Equal division is often appropriate. It is not the only thoughtful answer.

One child may have special needs. Another may have worked in the family business. One may have received substantial lifetime assistance. One may want the family home while the others prefer liquid assets. Pretax and after-tax assets may also carry different economic value.

If distributions are unequal, understand why and consider whether communicating the reasoning could reduce later conflict. Insurance can sometimes equalize an inheritance when a business or property passes to one beneficiary.

Be intentional. Silence leaves survivors to explain your decision with incomplete information and fully developed emotions.

Charitable Legacy Can Improve the Tax Result

A church, charity, or other qualified organization generally does not pay income tax on pretax retirement assets. Family beneficiaries usually do. That difference can make traditional retirement accounts efficient charitable assets while other property passes to people.

A charitable beneficiary designation, donor-advised fund, charitable trust, life-insurance gift, or qualified charitable distribution during life may support different goals. Each carries distinct legal, tax, control, and administrative considerations.

Lifetime giving lets the retiree see the impact, involve family, and align money with values now. Testamentary giving can preserve resources for lifetime needs while creating a future gift.

Do not let tax efficiency choose a cause you do not care about. Start with generosity; then improve how it is delivered.

Your Digital Estate and Federal Access

Email, cloud storage, photographs, social media, websites, subscriptions, cryptocurrency, electronic statements, and password systems are part of modern estate administration.

Your survivor may need email access to locate OPM notices, TSP communications, insurance records, and tax documents. Service-provider agreements and state fiduciary-access laws can govern what an agent or executor may access.

Use a secure password manager or documented access system, not a plain-text password list taped beneath the keyboard. Record where credentials, recovery codes, devices, and digital instructions are maintained.

Digital organization is not glamorous. Neither is spending six hours trying to recover an email account while the utility company continues its cheerful autopay schedule.

Do Not Create a Federal-Benefits Treasure Hunt

Build an 'If Something Happens' file that the right people can actually locate. Chapter 9 introduced the survivor file; the estate plan completes it.

Include the estate attorney, financial planner, tax professional, insurance contacts, account inventory, OPM claim information, FEHB or PSHB records, Medicare information, FEGLI, TSP, Social Security, pensions, debts, deeds, business interests, funeral wishes, pet instructions, and digital-access plan.

Keep sensitive information secure and tell trusted people how access works. Review the file annually and after major changes.

Organization is one of the least expensive—and most compassionate—estate-planning tools available.

Teach Before You Transfer

A federal employee can spend a career accumulating pension rights and TSP wealth, then transfer the account to someone who has never managed more than a checking account.

Talk with adult children about investing, taxes, debt, generosity, scams, and what the family wealth represents. Introduce the spouse and appropriate family members to the professional team before a crisis.

The first meeting with the financial planner should not be scheduled between the funeral and the reading of a suspiciously old beneficiary form.

The greatest inheritance may include both resources and the judgment to use them well.

The Ethical Will

Your estate transfers property. Your legacy transfers meaning.

An ethical will is not a legal document and does not distribute assets. It is a letter, recording, or collection of stories communicating values, faith, lessons, hopes, family history, apologies, gratitude, and love.

Explain why you saved, what you sacrificed, what you learned, and what you hope the opportunity will make possible. A grandchild may remember the story behind the account long after forgetting its opening balance.

A financial statement can measure an estate. It cannot measure the example that created it.

Specialized Coordination Matters

Federal estate planning crosses federal benefit rules, state property law, retirement-account taxation, insurance, Social Security, and family dynamics.

A Chartered Federal Employee Benefits Consultant℠ (ChFEBC℠) has specialized training in federal employee benefits and can help coordinate the federal records with the financial plan. An estate-planning attorney drafts and interprets legal documents; a tax professional addresses tax law; other specialists may be needed for business, special-needs, elder-law, or charitable planning.

No credential replaces current verification. Federal procedures, tax rules, family circumstances, and state law change.

The plan works when every professional and every document is solving the same problem for the same people.

Legacy Begins Before Death

The most meaningful use of wealth may happen while you are present to witness it: a family trip, education, help with a first home, generosity, time with grandchildren, or support for a cause.

That does not mean giving away money needed for retirement, survivor security, or care. It means recognizing that legacy is not limited to the remainder after every living opportunity has passed.

Take care of your life. Protect those who depend on you. Then use what remains—during life and after it—with intention.

Money is a tool for meaning. Estate planning makes sure the tool does not lose its instructions when you are no longer there to explain them.

Your Purpose Driven Federal Employee Action Step

Build the Federal Estate Coordination Map. Complete the legal plan and the benefit records as one project.

Purpose statement Write what you want to protect and what remaining wealth should accomplish.

Legal documents Review the will, trust, financial power of attorney, healthcare documents, guardians, executors, trustees, and successors with qualified counsel.

Federal forms Verify TSP, FEGLI, FERS or CSRS retirement-contribution, and unpaid-compensation beneficiary records using current procedures.

Survivor record Confirm the OPM survivor election, FEHB or PSHB continuation plan, former-spouse orders, and current marital information.

After-tax inheritance Estimate beneficiary taxes and distribution deadlines for traditional TSP, Roth, taxable assets, insurance, and charitable gifts.

Complete the Family and Legacy Review

Special circumstances Address minors, special needs, blended families, businesses, real estate in multiple states, creditor concerns, and charitable intentions.

Asset alignment Confirm titles, trust funding, payable-on-death and transfer-on-death arrangements, and insurance ownership match the legal plan.

Digital access Document accounts, devices, password-management access, recovery instructions, and authority for digital property.

Family meeting Explain roles, unusual decisions, document location, professional contacts, and the first calls to make.

Legacy record Write an ethical will, preserve stories, and identify meaningful gifts or experiences you want to create during life.

The estate plan is complete only when the legal documents, federal records, tax strategy, and family understanding all tell the same story. The goal is not merely to transfer property. It is to protect people and transfer purpose.

Chapter 12

What Are You Retiring To?

We have spent eleven chapters building the machinery: eligibility, pension income, the supplement, Social Security, TSP, FEHB, Medicare, taxes, survivor protection, long-term care, and estate planning.

That work matters. But now imagine the first ordinary Monday after retirement. Nobody expects you at the agency. There is no commute, staff call, suspense date, conference line, leave request, or calendar invitation labeled 'quick touch base' that somehow occupies fifty-eight minutes.

For decades, that freedom sounded wonderful. For a while, it probably will be. Then another question appears: What am I going to do today?

Financial planning can help you become free to retire. It cannot decide what you will do with the freedom. The real question is not merely what you are retiring from. It is what you are retiring to.

The Federal Identity Shift

Career federal employees often carry more than a job title. They carry a mission, an oath, a clearance, an agency culture, specialized knowledge, and an identity built around public service.

People may have introduced you by the work: investigator, engineer, analyst, scientist, firefighter, officer, administrator, physician, manager, or the person who could finally explain what the regulation meant. Then the badge is returned, the email account disappears, and someone else sits in the chair.

That transition can create pride, relief, grief, uncertainty, and excitement at the same time. Missing parts of the work does not mean retirement was a mistake. Feeling ready to leave does not erase the meaning of the service.

Give yourself permission to honor the identity you built without requiring it to be the only identity you keep.

The Monday Morning Problem

Work provides more than pay. It provides structure, deadlines, progress, colleagues, recognition, and the reassuring evidence that somebody needs you somewhere at 8:30.

Retirement removes much of that structure at once. At first you sleep later, travel, complete house projects, and enjoy the radical act of visiting the grocery store when nobody else is there.

Eventually, every day can begin to feel like Saturday. Saturday is less thrilling when it happens seven times a week.

The Monday Morning Problem is not a financial shortfall. It is the challenge of creating rhythm, meaning, and connection after the institution no longer supplies them.

Retirement Is a Gift of Time

During a career, money feels scarce. Yet time is the resource continuously leaving the account: workdays, commutes, travel, late emails, emergency calls, and mental space occupied by tomorrow's problem.

Retirement can return thousands of hours each year. A person retiring at sixty may receive decades in which more of the calendar belongs to them.

That is an extraordinary form of wealth. Like money, it can be spent intentionally, wasted accidentally, invested in relationships, donated to others, or saved for a someday that never arrives.

Your pension and TSP purchase control over time. The life plan decides whether that purchase was worth making.

Build a Life Plan Beside the Financial Plan

Federal employees are used to plans with forms, dates, signatures, and instructions written as though punctuation required legal review. A retirement life plan can be simpler.

What do you want to see, learn, experience, build, repair, create, teach, give, and become? Who deserves more of your time? Which relationships need attention? What did you postpone because the mission, travel schedule, or commute kept winning?

Write the answers. A goal that remains only in conversation is easy to postpone. A goal placed beside the financial projection can receive time, money, and a date.

Your allocation of years deserves at least as much thought as your allocation of funds.

The Bucket List Is a Living Tool

A bucket list is often treated as a catalog of spectacular things to complete before death: see the Northern Lights, visit every national park, attend the Masters, learn guitar, take the family to Italy, write a book, or drive across the country.

Those goals are wonderful. But the list should not be completed once, placed in a drawer, and rediscovered when the passport expires.

Use it throughout retirement. Add goals, remove goals that no longer matter, revise them as health and family change, and return to the list whenever the calendar begins filling with other people's priorities.

The bucket list is not a scorecard of expensive experiences. It is a recurring reminder of what you said you wanted your time and resources to accomplish.

The Buried Life Question

Years ago, MTV aired The Buried Life, a show built around four young men pursuing one hundred things they wanted to do before they died.

The idea included a second question. As they pursued their own goals, they helped other people accomplish theirs.

That combination is a strong retirement philosophy: What do I want to experience, and whose life can I help make better?

A purpose-driven list should include adventure and contribution. Retirement can give you both the time to live more of your own story and the capacity to enter someone else's story at exactly the right moment.

Make a Big List and an Everyday List

The Big List contains the experiences you would genuinely regret missing: the journey, celebration, family gathering, creative project, or personal challenge that matters deeply.

The Everyday List gives an ordinary week rhythm: walk four mornings, read each month, breakfast with a friend on Tuesday, volunteer twice a month, take one grandchild somewhere, learn a skill, grow tomatoes, attend worship, or call someone who needs company.

Big goals create milestones. Small practices create a life. Antarctica may be memorable, but it cannot tell you what to do next Wednesday.

Build both lists. Retirement needs mountain peaks and a pleasant trail between them.

Purpose Does Not Have to Be Grand

Purpose does not require starting a foundation, writing a bestseller, or solving a national problem you spent thirty years watching survive every task force.

It may mean becoming the grandparent who attends the games, making breakfast for your spouse, tending a garden, serving at church, walking the dog, mentoring one person, caring for a neighbor, or being available when somebody needs to talk.

Purpose is not measured by the size of the audience. It is the experience of knowing your time matters.

You can retire from a position without retiring from usefulness.

Create the Ordinary April Calendar

Imagine a normal month in retirement. Not Christmas. Not the family cruise. Just April.

What happens Monday through Friday? Where do health, friendships, family, faith, learning, service, recreation, household work, and rest appear? Which activities require other people, reservations, or recurring commitments?

The goal is not to rebuild the federal workweek with yourself as both employee and supervisor. It is to create enough structure that time supports the life you want.

A blank calendar can feel like freedom. Thirty blank years can feel like something else.

Do Not Overschedule Freedom

Some retirees solve the open calendar by accepting every committee, consulting request, childcare assignment, board seat, trip, club, and volunteer role placed before them.

Soon they are busier than before retirement, except the new organization lacks a pension and has discovered they answer email quickly.

Retirement should contain empty space: coffee without a deadline, spontaneous travel, rest, unplanned afternoons, and the ability to say yes when something meaningful appears.

Purpose and freedom can coexist. The goal is not to fill every hour. It is to keep years from passing unintentionally.

Retirement Changes the Household

One person's retirement also changes the spouse's life. The retiree is now home more often, using shared space, changing routines, and possibly developing informed opinions about how the dishwasher has historically been loaded.

Discuss expectations before the retirement date. How much time will you spend together and separately? Who handles household responsibilities? How will caregiving, travel, grandchildren, hobbies, and personal space work?

If one spouse continues working, retirement can create different schedules and different ideas about discretionary spending. Neither person's calendar automatically becomes the other's property.

A retirement plan should protect the relationship, not merely place two financially secure people in the same kitchen all day.

The First Ten Years Are Not Interchangeable

The early years of retirement may offer more mobility, energy, health, and confidence. Later years can still be rich and meaningful, but they may support different goals.

If a dream requires hiking, long flights, lifting grandchildren, driving an RV, or tolerating an airport connection designed by someone who dislikes people, consider doing it sooner.

Some family windows are time-sensitive too. Grandchildren grow. Parents age. Friends move. A spouse's health can change. Money may wait; the people and ability involved may not.

Stage the bucket list according to energy and relationships—not merely account balances.

Turn 'Someday' Into a Planning Period

Someday we will visit Italy. Someday I will write the book. Someday we will rent the RV, take Dad fishing, learn piano, volunteer, or get healthier.

Someday is patient. It will allow itself to be postponed indefinitely without complaint.

Place each important goal into a period: before retirement, the first year, years one through five, years six through ten, or later. Exact dates can come afterward.

Once a dream enters the timeline, the financial plan can fund it and the calendar can protect it.

Put a Price Beside the Dream

Some goals cost almost nothing. Others require serious money. Estimate the amount without apologizing for the experience.

'Discretionary spending: $20,000' is abstract. 'Take the entire family on a trip while the grandchildren are still young' is an assignment. The same withdrawal feels different when its purpose is visible.

Include travel, vehicles, hobbies, education, gifts, charitable work, home projects, and family experiences in the retirement cash-flow plan. Decide which expenses repeat and which occur once.

A projection should not merely prove the portfolio survives. It should show whether the life you described has been funded.

Give the Annual-Leave Check a Job

Many federal employees receive a lump-sum payment for accumulated annual leave after separation. The check can feel like a retirement bonus, but it is generally taxable compensation and may arrive on a schedule the retiree does not control.

Decide its job in advance. It might fund the income gap while OPM finalizes the annuity, replenish cash reserves, pay taxes, eliminate debt, or finance a first-year bucket-list goal.

Do not spend the same leave payment three times in the mental plan. A dollar can fund the bridge, the cruise, or the new kitchen. Even a federal dollar has not been trained to do all three simultaneously.

Coordinate withholding and liquidity so the first months of retirement feel intentional rather than improvised.

Post-Retirement Work Needs a Purpose Too

Some federal retirees want consulting, part-time work, a second career, teaching, or service with another organization. Work can provide structure, social connection, meaning, and income.

Define why you are doing it. Is the income necessary, useful for a goal, or simply pleasant? How many hours are you willing to sell? What freedom must remain protected?

Federal retirees considering reemployment with the government should understand how the position may affect annuity payments, pay, benefits, and taxes. Agency authorities and individual arrangements can differ, so verify the rules before accepting the role.

Retiring from one job only to become trapped in a second one with worse parking is not automatically progress.

Use the One-Year List

A thirty-year vision can feel abstract. Create a list for the next twelve months.

Choose ten items: visit somewhere new, reconnect with a friend, learn something, improve health, do something with a child or grandchild, serve, repair a relationship, try something uncomfortable, help another person accomplish a goal, and do one thing purely for joy.

Add dates or seasons. Put the first actions on the calendar. Estimate the cost and identify who should join you.

Purpose becomes real when the next step occurs before the next annual review.

Purpose Changes With the Retirement Seasons

Purpose at sixty may not be purpose at eighty. The active years may emphasize travel, adventure, work, and learning. The steady years may emphasize family, community, mentoring, and service. The support years may emphasize connection, storytelling, giving, and presence.

Changing the plan is not failure. A list should serve the life—not require the life to serve an old list.

Review goals alongside health, housing, spending, investments, and care planning. Retirements evolve because people do.

The constant is not the activity. It is the intention to use time in a way that still matters.

Do Not Wait for Retirement to Begin Living

Retirement planning should prepare tomorrow without consuming every meaningful part of today.

If something matters deeply and can be done responsibly now, consider doing it. Take the trip, call the friend, spend time with family, improve health, begin learning, or start serving.

A later retirement with a slightly larger account is not automatically better than a well-planned retirement that begins while the people and abilities required are still present.

The financial plan should protect the future. It should not hold the present hostage.

Apply the Purpose Test

For every major retirement decision, ask: Does this help us live the retirement we said we wanted?

Should we buy the vacation home? Does it support the life or create an obligation? Should we work two more years? Does the additional security outweigh what is postponed? Should we fund the family trip? Does it create the experience we value without threatening independence?

Should we take more investment risk? Is the risk needed for the goals, or are we protecting a scoreboard? Should we help a child? Does the gift express our values while preserving our own plan?

Purpose gives financial decisions something more useful to measure than net worth alone.

Create a New Scoreboard

Career success may have been measured by grade, title, awards, promotions, responsibility, mission completion, salary, or how many acronyms you could use without explanation.

Retirement permits a different scoreboard: days with grandchildren, meals shared, miles walked, friendships maintained, people helped, books read, skills learned, faith deepened, money given, memories created, and years of independence preserved.

These measures are not less serious because they do not appear on an SF form. They may be the clearest evidence that the retirement plan worked.

You spent decades accumulating resources so that one day you could own more of your time. Decide what success looks like now that the time is yours.

Do Not Retire From Purpose

Retirement is not the end of usefulness or the waiting room at the end of life. For many people, it is the first season in which they control a meaningful share of their time, resources, relationships, and contribution.

You can retire from an agency, position, schedule, or career. You do not need to retire from curiosity, service, growth, connection, or purpose.

The pension, TSP, and health benefits are not the retirement. They are the tools that help make the retirement possible.

The question behind this entire book remains: Now that you have worked for the life, what will you do with it?

Your Purpose Driven Federal Employee Action Step

Create the Purpose Driven Retirement Roadmap and revisit it throughout life—not only during the year you separate from service.

Big list Write the experiences you would deeply regret never pursuing.

Everyday list Choose recurring practices that give ordinary weeks health, connection, service, learning, joy, and rhythm.

Categories Add at least three ideas under adventure, family, relationships, health, learning, faith, service, creation, giving, and just for fun.

Priority ten Circle the ten items that matter most in the current season.

Timing Place each priority before retirement, in year one, years one through five, years six through ten, or later.

Complete the Time and Purpose Review

People Identify who should share each experience and whether the plan has been discussed with them.

Cost Estimate the amount, frequency, and funding source for each goal.

Calendar Design an ordinary April with enough structure for purpose and enough open space for freedom.

One-year plan Choose ten actions for the next twelve months and schedule the first step for each.

Purpose test Review major work, spending, housing, investment, and family decisions against the retirement you said you wanted.

A successful federal retirement is not measured only by whether every benefit was calculated correctly. It is measured by whether those benefits helped you use your time, health, relationships, and resources for a life you were genuinely glad to live.

Chapter 13

Retirement Changes Your Relationships Too

Retirement changes your schedule, income, identity, and daily routine. Very often, it also changes your relationships.

For decades, work organized the household. You left, returned, traveled, took calls, handled emergencies, and spent more waking hours with certain coworkers than with members of your own family. Your spouse had a routine. You had a routine. The agency had approximately seventeen routines for requesting leave.

Then retirement arrives. Suddenly, the people in the household have more time together—and different ideas about how that time should be used.

Retirement is not only a financial transition. It is a relationship transition. Like every other important part of retirement, it works better when the expectations are discussed before they become grievances.

'You're Home Again?'

One spouse retires. Both have looked forward to it for years. A few weeks later, someone wonders—quietly at first—whether the retiree intends to be in the kitchen all day.

Nothing terrible happened. Two routines collided. One spouse imagined travel, long walks, lunches, and family time. The other imagined golf, projects, sleeping later, hobbies, or a quiet house in which nobody offers operational feedback on folding towels.

Neither vision is wrong. They are simply different.

Couples should ask more than, 'When can we retire?' They should ask, 'What does each of us believe retirement will look like after the celebration ends?'

Shared Purpose and Individual Purpose

A strong retirement does not require spouses to do everything together. It may be healthier when they do not.

The household may share priorities around travel, grandchildren, faith, charitable giving, health, housing, and family. Each spouse may also have separate interests, friendships, projects, and needs for solitude or activity.

One may love golf while the other regards four hours watching someone search for a ball as an inefficient use of daylight. One may want constant travel while the other genuinely likes home.

A healthy retirement can include our purpose and my purpose. Independence can make shared time more interesting, not less loving.

Do Not Make Your Spouse the Entire Plan

Your spouse may be your favorite person. That does not mean they should become your only friend, hobby, activity partner, social connection, and source of purpose.

That is a large assignment for one human—particularly one who did not receive a position description or locality pay.

Friends, learning, exercise, service, hobbies, and personal goals allow each spouse to keep growing. They also bring new stories and energy back into the relationship.

A marriage can be the center of retirement without becoming the entire circumference.

The Conversation Most Couples Never Have

Each spouse should separately describe an ideal retirement week. Then compare the answers.

How much time do you expect to spend together? How much do you want alone? How often will you travel? Will you move? What role will children and grandchildren play? How much financial help should family receive? What does a relaxing day actually mean?

Discuss household work, caregiving, hobbies, friends, faith, sleep schedules, and spending. Ask what each person fears retirement may change about the relationship.

Agreement is helpful. Discovering disagreement early may be even more helpful, because expectations can be negotiated before they become evidence in an argument.

One Retirement Date May Not Fit Two People

In a dual-career household, spouses may not retire together. One may be older, healthier, more satisfied at work, or eligible for a different pension and health-benefit arrangement.

When both are federal employees, separate service histories, retirement systems, FEHB or PSHB records, TSP balances, survivor elections, and Social Security situations can produce different ideal dates. 'We started together' is not a benefit formula.

A staggered retirement can preserve income, insurance options, and savings while giving the first retiree time to adjust. It can also create tension if the retired spouse expects the working spouse to adopt a retirement schedule prematurely.

Model the benefits, then discuss the life. The best household date may be two dates coordinated around one shared plan.

Work Used to Hide Differences

Work creates structure and separation. Two people can maintain very different routines without noticing because much of the week is already occupied.

Retirement makes differences more visible: sleep, spending, social needs, travel, household standards, support for adult children, location, television volume, and whether 'doing nothing' is restful or alarming.

Differences do not automatically create problems. Assuming the other person sees retirement exactly as you do often does.

Curiosity is usually more useful than persuasion. Ask what the preference protects: security, freedom, family, identity, comfort, adventure, or control.

Money Becomes Emotional in a New Way

One spouse may be comfortable spending while the other fears running out. One says, 'We worked for this.' The other says, 'We do not know what could happen.'

Both are often protecting something important. One protects experiences; the other protects security.

A well-built income and tax plan can establish what is safely available for lifestyle goals, what must remain for care and survival, and which expenses require a separate decision.

The plan becomes a neutral reference rather than a contestant in the argument.

A TSP balance is not a relationship strategy. Two people need a shared understanding of what the account is allowed—and expected—to do.

Give the Money Purpose Together

Instead of asking, 'Why do you want to spend $15,000 on that?' ask, 'Does this support something we agreed matters?'

Instead of, 'Why are we helping the children again?' ask whether the assistance expresses shared values without threatening independence, survivor security, or long-term care.

Purpose turns spending from a contest between saver and spender into a decision about priorities. It also makes saying no easier when an expense does not support the plan.

The goal is not for one spouse to win. It is for the money to serve the household both people are trying to protect.

Friendships Change After Federal Service

Federal work creates built-in relationships through teams, field offices, details, training, deployments, investigations, projects, and the shared experience of explaining your agency to relatives who remain unconvinced it exists.

Some friendships continue after retirement. Many fade when the workplace no longer supplies proximity and common problems. That is not necessarily betrayal. It is often geography and routine doing what they do.

Decide which relationships deserve effort. Exchange personal contact information before the government email account closes. Schedule the lunch instead of saying everyone should 'definitely stay in touch.'

Retirement requires social infrastructure just as surely as it requires income infrastructure.

Isolation Is a Retirement Risk

Market declines, inflation, taxes, and healthcare are visible planning risks. Isolation belongs on the list too.

It can follow retirement, relocation, hearing or mobility loss, caregiving, the death of a spouse, or the gradual loss of friends. A person may be financially secure and profoundly alone.

Connection supports meaning, accountability, activity, and the simple reassurance that someone would notice if you did not arrive. Relationships are not a decorative addition to the retirement plan.

If people matter, put them on the calendar. What is not scheduled is often surrendered to convenience.

Put People on the Calendar

Schedule lunch with friends, family dinners, worship, clubs, volunteer groups, grandchildren, travel companions, and recurring calls.

Some relationships thrive on spontaneity. Most also benefit from somebody choosing a date.

Create regular points of connection during the ordinary months—not only holidays and emergencies. Include people of different ages and communities so the social world does not depend entirely on one circle aging together.

Retirement gives you greater control of time. Use some of that control to protect the people who make the time worth having.

When One Spouse Wants to Move

One spouse wants warmth, low taxes, and less maintenance. The other wants grandchildren, familiar doctors, friends, church, seasons, and the home where the family grew up.

This is not merely a housing decision. Each person may be protecting belonging, adventure, financial security, identity, care access, or family.

Test alternatives: seasonal living, extended rentals, downsizing nearby, moving closer but not next door, or delaying the decision. Evaluate taxes, healthcare, transportation, airports, community, insurance, and what happens after the first death.

The mathematically cheapest location is not automatically the place where two people will build their best life.

The House Is More Than an Asset

A financial plan sees equity, taxes, maintenance, and opportunity cost. A family sees holidays, height marks, pets, neighbors, a spouse's favorite chair, and a lifetime of ordinary memories.

Remaining in the home can be an entirely valid use of money when it is sustainable and compatible with aging. Downsizing can also release time, capital, and energy for other priorities.

Discuss the emotional and practical value. Consider accessibility, care, transportation, survivor manageability, maintenance, and proximity to people—not appreciation alone.

Optimization is a tool. It should not bulldoze purpose simply because the spreadsheet found a cheaper zip code.

Create Three Bucket Lists

Take Chapter 12's living bucket list and create three versions: My List, Your List, and Our List.

The exercise may reveal a dream your spouse has never mentioned, a goal one person assumed was shared, or a priority appearing on both lists that deserves immediate attention.

Place dates, costs, and names beside the shared goals. Protect individual goals with time and reasonable funding too.

Aligned priorities do not require identical calendars. They require mutual respect for what gives each person's time meaning.

Try the One-Yes Rule

Each year, allow each spouse to choose one significant, reasonable item from the personal list. The other agrees to support it when the financial and practical plan permits.

It may be a trip, class, project, event, experience, volunteer commitment, or purchase tied to a real goal.

You do not need to share your spouse's enthusiasm for pottery, fly-fishing, genealogy, or a carefully restored vehicle with no cup holders. You can still support the dream.

Helping someone you love live more fully can become part of your own purpose.

Adult Children and Financial Help

Retirement can change the family's expectations around money and availability. Adult children may need help with education, housing, childcare, emergencies, business ideas, or debt.

Decide what the household wants to support and what it does not. Distinguish gifts that create opportunity from repeated assistance that weakens the retiree's independence or the child's responsibility.

Coordinate gifts with taxes, estate plans, long-term care, survivor needs, and fairness among children. Do not promise money from a traditional TSP without calculating the taxes required to produce the desired net gift.

Generosity is most sustainable when it has boundaries and both spouses understand them.

Grandchildren Are Not a Retirement Schedule

Grandchildren can be one of retirement's greatest joys. They can also become an unspoken expectation that the retired grandparents are permanently available.

Discuss childcare, school pickups, travel, expenses, discipline, privacy, and how much time each spouse genuinely wants to commit. Loving grandchildren does not require abandoning every individual plan.

Create experiences intentionally: one-on-one days, traditions, trips, lessons, stories, and time that builds relationships rather than merely fills logistical gaps.

Grandparents can be generous and present without becoming the family's unpaid department of transportation.

Retirement Can Strengthen a Marriage

The transition has challenges, but it also offers extraordinary opportunity: breakfasts, travel, conversation, exercise, shared projects, intimacy, family, spontaneity, and less work stress.

Many couples spent decades building a life while managing careers, children, mortgages, school schedules, and caregiving. Retirement may be the first time in years that a large portion of the calendar truly belongs to them.

Use that gift deliberately. Create rituals, pursue shared goals, protect individual growth, and continue dating the person who has now seen your full weekday routine.

A stronger relationship is not an automatic retirement benefit. It is one of the best benefits the household can intentionally build.

Build a Life That Can Survive Loss

For many couples, one spouse will eventually live part of retirement alone. Chapter 9 prepared the finances. The human plan matters too.

If your spouse died first, who would you call, see, serve, and spend time with? Which activities would remain? Could you manage the home? Would you have transportation, community, faith, friends, and a reason to get up tomorrow?

A resilient life has multiple sources of meaning: spouse, family, friends, faith, health, learning, service, hobbies, and community. When one changes, the others can still support the person.

That is not emotional pessimism. It is life diversification.

Use the Annual Relationship Check-In

Once each year, ask: Are you enjoying retirement? What should we do more or less? Do you have enough independence? Are we aligned on money, housing, family, and travel? Are we postponing something important?

Also ask what has changed. Health, grief, energy, friendships, grandchildren, caregiving, and purpose can change the answer from one year to the next.

Listen without immediately solving. Some concerns need empathy before they need an action item—a concept that may feel unfamiliar after a career of meetings.

Small conversations held regularly can prevent years of quiet frustration.

Relationships Are Retirement Assets

Pensions, TSP accounts, homes, insurance, and investments appear on statements. Relationships do not.

Yet relationships may determine whether retirement feels rich, connected, safe, and meaningful—or empty. They require deposits of time, attention, forgiveness, presence, and shared experience.

When people identify what matters most, they rarely begin with an account balance. They name a spouse, family, faith, freedom, health, and the ability to help others.

The money expands the ability to act on those priorities. It should never distract from why they were priorities in the first place.

Protect the People, Not Just the Plan

The purpose of retirement planning is not to construct a technically perfect financial machine. It is to support people—including you.

If every benefit election is correct but the household never discussed how it wants to live, something important remains unfinished.

Measure success broadly: not only 'Do we have enough?' but 'Are we using our time, money, and freedom to strengthen what matters most?'

That question leads naturally to another retirement asset that cannot be replaced once it is gone: health.

Your Purpose Driven Federal Employee Action Step

Complete the Retirement Relationship Plan individually first, then compare the answers without assuming difference means disloyalty.

Ideal week Describe how much shared time, independent time, activity, rest, and social connection each person expects.

Three lists Complete My List, Your List, and Our List; identify the shared goals that deserve dates and funding.

Money Agree on lifestyle spending, reserves, family assistance, large purchases, and the purpose of TSP withdrawals.

Retirement dates If both spouses work, determine whether coordinated but different dates better serve benefits and life.

Home Discuss location, family proximity, accessibility, maintenance, climate, community, and the survivor's ability to remain.

Complete the Family and Connection Review

Family roles Set expectations for adult children, grandchildren, aging parents, caregiving, time, and financial support.

Friendships Identify five people each spouse wants to remain close to and schedule recurring contact.

Individual purpose Confirm that each person has relationships and meaningful activity independent of the spouse.

First-death life Describe the survivor's likely housing, community, activities, transportation, and sources of purpose.

Annual conversation Schedule a yearly relationship review alongside the financial and benefit review.

A federal retirement can be perfectly calculated and still feel poor if the relationships around it are neglected. Invest in the people with the same intention you used to build the pension and TSP. They are the assets most likely to determine whether the years feel worthwhile.

Chapter 14

Your Health Is Retirement Capital

We have spent much of this book inventorying assets: the FERS or CSRS pension, TSP, Social Security, FEHB or PSHB, savings, investments, insurance, and the home.

There is another retirement asset that appears on no federal statement: your health.

Imagine reaching retirement with every financial box checked and an ambitious bucket list—travel, national parks, grandchildren, golf, mission trips, family vacations—only to discover that your body can no longer do most of it. Financially, the plan succeeded. Practically, much of the freedom is difficult to use.

Money gives you the financial ability to do things. Health gives you the physical and mental ability to experience them. A Purpose Driven Federal Retirement needs both.

Healthspan Matters

Financial plans ask how long retirement may last. That is lifespan. A life plan should also ask how many of those years are likely to remain active, independent, and usable. That is healthspan.

Two retirees may both live to ninety-two. One remains engaged and mobile until ninety. The other experiences serious limitations beginning at seventy-two. The lifespans match; the retirements do not.

No plan can guarantee healthspan. Genetics, illness, accidents, occupation, access to care, and circumstances matter. Yet many daily choices can support strength, mobility, prevention, sleep, connection, and mental wellbeing.

The financial plan prepares for a long life. The personal plan tries to preserve as much life as possible within those years.

Go Back to the Bucket List

Review the living bucket list from Chapter 12. Beside each goal, write what your body and mind must be capable of doing.

Walking through Rome requires mobility and endurance. Golf at seventy-five requires strength, balance, and rotation. A day at Disney with grandchildren requires more steps than several government fitness tests. Remaining at home requires the ability to navigate, carry, rise, reach, and recover safely.

International travel may involve luggage, stairs, unfamiliar food, medication management, long flights, and airports in which the correct gate is apparently assigned after consulting a random-number generator.

Exercise and healthcare become more meaningful when connected to a person, place, and experience you care about.

Train for the Retirement You Described

People train for races, competitions, deployments, physical standards, and demanding assignments. Why not train for retirement?

The goal is not to become twenty-five again. It is to remain capable of living the life you chose for as long as reasonably possible.

You may be training for Italy, golf, gardening, grandchildren, travel, independence, your spouse, or the ability to get off the floor without converting the moment into a family meeting.

Work with appropriate medical and fitness professionals, especially when conditions, medications, injuries, or limitations are present. This chapter offers a planning framework—not individualized medical advice.

Unused Sick Leave Is Not Health Capital

Federal employees may accumulate large sick-leave balances. Under applicable retirement rules, unused sick leave can increase service used in the annuity computation. It generally cannot make someone eligible to retire, and it is not paid as a cash balance at separation.

That service credit can improve the pension. It cannot retroactively replace preventive care, rehabilitation, sleep, movement, or treatment postponed during the career.

Use sick leave appropriately when health requires it. Follow agency policy and medical guidance. Preserving every hour while ignoring a legitimate problem can be an expensive way to add a modest amount to the annuity.

Sick leave is a federal benefit. Health is the capacity the benefit was designed to help protect.

You Cannot Buy Yesterday's Health

A financial shortfall discovered at sixty-five may still have possible responses: work longer, spend less, move, adjust goals, or use assets differently.

You cannot return to forty-five and sleep, move, eat, recover, or attend appointments differently. The past is not available for a revised election.

That does not mean improvement is impossible later. People can gain strength, mobility, knowledge, and healthier routines at many ages with appropriate guidance.

It means health deserves attention before retirement with the same seriousness given to TSP contributions. Do not spend forty years funding a future while ignoring the person scheduled to arrive in it.

Strength Is an Independence Asset

Strength training may bring athletes or bodybuilders to mind. In retirement, strength becomes highly practical.

Can you carry groceries, lift a suitcase, rise from a chair, climb stairs, handle household tasks, work in the yard, play with grandchildren, and recover from a stumble?

Muscle and strength can support function, bone health, balance, metabolism, and independence, but the appropriate program depends on the individual. Medical clearance and qualified instruction may be important.

The goal is not a trophy. It is the ability to keep making ordinary choices without requiring someone else's assistance.

Mobility Is Freedom

Much of retirement depends on moving through the world: airports, sidewalks, beaches, stadiums, cars, houses, churches, museums, gardens, and grandchildren's events.

When mobility narrows, the world can become smaller. Social contact, confidence, travel, and independence may narrow with it.

Walking, mobility work, physical therapy, appropriate exercise, weight management, pain care, and accessible environments can each play a role depending on the person.

Maintaining movement is not merely a fitness objective. It is an options objective.

Balance Deserves a Line in the Plan

A stumble when young may create embarrassment. A fall later can create injury, hospitalization, rehabilitation, fear, and a lasting loss of independence.

Balance, vision, hearing, medication effects, footwear, home hazards, strength, and neurological or cardiovascular conditions can all matter. A qualified professional can help evaluate individual risks.

Review lighting, rugs, stairs, bathrooms, railings, and the places where movement has become uncertain. Asking for help early can preserve more freedom than pretending the concern is not there.

The objective is not extreme fitness. It is staying capable and safe enough to keep participating.

Do Not Retire Into the Recliner

Even desk jobs contain incidental movement: parking lots, hallways, stairs, lunch, meetings, and the long walk to a conference room someone booked in a different building.

Retirement can remove that movement overnight. No commute, workplace, errands tied to the workday, or reason to leave the house on certain mornings.

Choose activity you can sustain: walking, gardening, swimming, cycling, strength work, hiking, golf, pickleball, classes, dancing, or something else appropriate and enjoyable.

The best activity is often not the one an article ranks first. It is the safe one you will actually continue doing.

Health Needs a Calendar

Do not say, 'I will exercise when I have time.' Retirement has solved the scheduling mystery. The remaining question is whether time will be assigned.

Place movement, strength, appointments, sleep, meal planning, social connection, and recovery into the ordinary-April calendar. Build routines that survive travel, weather, and low motivation.

You scheduled meetings for an agency for decades. You can schedule a few recurring appointments with your future self—and this time the organizer may permit the meeting to end early.

Consistency matters more than a dramatic two-week campaign followed by a ceremonial return to the couch.

Preventive Care Is Maintenance

Most people maintain vehicles before they fail. They change oil, rotate tires, and investigate unfamiliar sounds rather than turning up the radio indefinitely.

Apply the same planning mindset to recommended physicals, screenings, dental care, vision, hearing, vaccinations, medication reviews, and follow-up. The appropriate schedule depends on age, history, risk, and professional guidance.

Federal employees in law enforcement, firefighting, military, healthcare, industrial, environmental, or other demanding roles may have occupational exposures or injuries worth discussing specifically with clinicians.

FEHB, PSHB, Medicare, and other insurance can help pay for covered care. Coverage is most useful when the person actually makes the appointment.

Know What Your Health Coverage Can—and Cannot—Do

FEHB or PSHB and Medicare can be powerful financial protections. They do not guarantee access to every provider, eliminate cost sharing, pay for every service, or create health through possession of an identification card.

Review networks, referrals, prescriptions, travel coverage, telehealth, rehabilitation, mental-health services, dental and vision arrangements, and coordination between Medicare and the federal plan. Revisit choices during Open Season and after major health changes.

Separate medical coverage from long-term custodial care, as Chapter 10 explained. Also maintain cash flow for deductibles, copayments, uncovered services, transportation, and support.

Good insurance protects the balance sheet. Good health planning helps the household use the insurance intelligently.

Put a Person Beside the Health Goal

'Stay healthy' is vague. Complete this sentence instead: I want to remain healthy enough to _____ with _____.

Travel with my spouse. Fish with my grandson. Dance at my granddaughter's wedding. Volunteer with my church. Take the family on a trip. Walk the city with friends. Remain at home with the person I love.

A person turns an abstract recommendation into a reason. The goal becomes connection rather than compliance.

That is the Purpose Driven difference: the habit serves a life, and the life supplies the motivation for the habit.

Mental Health Is Retirement Health

Retirement can bring relief and joy. It can also bring loss of identity, anxiety, grief, loneliness, depression, relationship strain, or the unsettling absence of structure.

Mental health deserves the same legitimacy as physical health. Speak with qualified professionals when symptoms, substance use, sleep, mood, trauma, or adjustment concerns interfere with life or safety.

Career federal employees may have experienced high-stress assignments, danger, repeated exposure to trauma, public scrutiny, or moral injury. Retirement does not require those experiences to disappear simply because the credential was returned.

Seeking support is not weakness. It is maintenance of an asset the entire retirement depends upon.

Keep the Mind Working

Work required learning, judgment, memory, communication, planning, problem solving, and adaptation. Retirement can remove much of that stimulation abruptly.

Read, study, take classes, write, travel, play music, build, teach, volunteer, learn technology, study faith or history, mentor, solve problems, and remain curious.

Cognitive health is influenced by many factors, and no activity guarantees a particular outcome. Engagement can still give the mind purpose and the days texture.

The career may end. Growth does not need to file a retirement application.

Sleep and Recovery Are Productive

A career may normalize short sleep, changing shifts, overnight calls, travel, stress, and the belief that exhaustion proves commitment.

Retirement offers an opportunity to rebuild consistent sleep and recovery. Persistent insomnia, snoring, breathing interruptions, daytime sleepiness, or other concerns deserve professional attention.

Rest is not laziness. It supports physical activity, mood, judgment, immune function, recovery, and the energy needed for relationships and purpose.

The goal is not to spend retirement asleep. It is to be awake enough to enjoy it.

Health and Wealth Can Work Together

Financial independence can create time and resources for healthier routines: better food, a trainer, therapy, equipment, a walkable community, transportation, home modifications, classes, or seasonal living that supports activity.

These are not automatically luxuries. Some are investments in capability, independence, and reduced burden on the family.

Evaluate spending by the Purpose Test. If a service helps preserve health needed for the retirement you described, it may deserve a clearer job in the budget.

The portfolio is not only there to produce statements. It can help construct an environment in which wellbeing is easier to maintain.

Health Changes the Financial Plan

A diagnosis, injury, disability, cognitive change, or caregiving need may affect retirement timing, work, travel, housing, Social Security, insurance, survivor elections, taxes, estate documents, and long-term care.

Update the plan when health changes. Revisit cash reserves, authorized decision-makers, insurance, account access, housing, income, and the burden placed on the spouse or family.

A plan created at sixty may need to look different at seventy-five. That is not failure. It is the plan responding to the person it exists to serve.

The most dangerous plan may be the one preserved perfectly after reality has changed.

Create the Retirement Capability List

Take the ten most important bucket-list items and identify the capabilities each requires: walking distance, stairs, balance, lifting, endurance, driving, hearing, vision, cognition, medication management, or emotional resilience.

Look for patterns. Those repeated capabilities become the practical health goals.

Then choose one current action with professional guidance as appropriate. Schedule the screening, begin the walking plan, address the pain, protect sleep, make the therapy appointment, or learn the exercise correctly.

Do not create twenty good intentions. Begin with one completed action. Action beats intention, including intention printed in an attractive workbook.

The Health Dividend

Investments can pay dividends. Health can too.

The dividend may be another trip, round of golf, year at home, afternoon with grandchildren, mission trip, drive to see a friend, walk on the beach, or morning in which ordinary tasks remain ordinary.

Those returns do not appear on a brokerage statement, but they are among the most valuable returns retirement capital can produce.

Do not measure health only in years. Measure independence, connection, experiences, contribution, and capability within the years.

Protect the Person Who Will Enjoy the Plan

The goal is not to live forever. None of us receives that election option.

The goal is to remain capable of living the chosen life for as long as reasonably possible, while adapting with dignity when circumstances change.

Your pension, TSP, Social Security, home, and insurance can fund retirement. Health, relationships, time, and purpose allow you to live it.

Do not spend the entire career building wealth and forget to protect the person who is supposed to enjoy it.

Your Purpose Driven Federal Employee Action Step

Build the Retirement Capability Plan with your healthcare and fitness professionals. Start with function and purpose, not a generic resolution.

Capability goals List what the ten highest-priority bucket-list items require your body and mind to do.

One action Choose one appropriate action to begin now and place it on the calendar.

Movement Identify physical activity you enjoy enough to sustain and obtain professional guidance when needed.

Strength and balance Evaluate how you will preserve functional strength, mobility, and fall resistance.

Preventive care Review recommended medical, dental, vision, hearing, vaccination, and occupational-exposure follow-up.

Complete the Coverage and Wellbeing Review

Mental wellbeing Create support for stress, mood, sleep, grief, trauma, identity transition, and social connection.

Coverage Review FEHB or PSHB, Medicare coordination, prescriptions, providers, rehabilitation, travel, and expected out-of-pocket costs.

Home Identify accessibility and safety changes that support mobility and independence.

People Complete: 'I want to remain healthy enough to _____ with _____.'

Plan update Define which health changes should trigger an immediate financial, legal, housing, or long-term-care review.

A strong retirement plan funds the future. A strong health plan preserves more of the person who will live it. Protect both forms of capital, because the return you truly want is not merely a larger account—it is another meaningful year with the ability to use it.

Chapter 15

Purpose Through Service, Giving, and Contribution

An interesting question sometimes appears after retirement: Does anybody still need me?

For decades, the answer was obvious. The agency needed you. Coworkers, citizens, leaders, employees, partners, and family needed you. There were deadlines, problems, responsibilities, and a mortgage that demonstrated unwavering confidence in your continued employment.

Then the paycheck stops, the calendar clears, and the phone rings less often. Freedom feels good, yet some retirees discover that being needed supplied something they did not fully appreciate while working: purpose.

One of retirement's most meaningful questions is not only, 'What do I want to do?' It is also, 'What can I still do for someone else?'

A Career in Public Service Leaves Something Behind

Federal employees spend careers serving a public mission, even when the daily work feels several layers removed from the public and alarmingly close to a spreadsheet.

You may have protected people, administered programs, maintained infrastructure, enforced laws, cared for veterans, managed resources, supported research, responded to disasters, or helped the government perform work most citizens never see.

Retirement ends the appointment. It does not erase the habits, judgment, technical knowledge, leadership, and service orientation built through the career.

Public service can continue without a federal title. Retirement gives you more freedom to choose the people and causes that receive it next.

You Have More to Give Than Money

Financial planning often describes giving through charitable gifts, qualified charitable distributions, donor-advised funds, appreciated securities, insurance, beneficiary designations, and estate plans.

Those tools matter. They represent only one form of generosity. You also possess time, knowledge, relationships, skills, wisdom, attention, credibility, and perspective earned through success, failure, leadership, loss, family, faith, and starting over.

Something that took twenty years to learn may save another person twenty months—or one terrible decision.

Retirement creates the opportunity to share capital that never appeared in the TSP.

Your Career Ends; Your Value Does Not

Our culture can present retirement as an expiration date: you contributed, received the plaque, ate the sheet cake, and should now move politely toward leisure.

Retiring from employment does not mean retiring from usefulness. It may create opportunities to contribute in ways the career's schedule, restrictions, and responsibilities never allowed.

During working years, a portion of your time belonged to the mission. In retirement, more of it belongs to you.

The question becomes: Who deserves that time now? Financial independence gives you the privilege of choosing the answer.

Contribution Does Not Need to Become Another Job

Purpose does not require retiring Friday and reporting to a nonprofit for forty hours on Monday. You are allowed to enjoy retirement.

Contribution might mean mentoring monthly, tutoring, serving at church, coaching, supporting veterans, joining a board, sharing professional expertise, helping a neighbor, watching grandchildren by agreement, or calling someone who is lonely.

A small recurring commitment can be more sustainable and meaningful than a heroic schedule that recreates the burnout retirement was supposed to solve.

The goal is not to remain busy. It is to remain connected to something larger than yourself.

Activity and Purpose Are Different

A retirement can be wonderfully busy: golf, pickleball, lunch, travel, clubs, projects, and dinner. Enjoyment belongs in the plan.

Activity answers, 'What am I doing?' Purpose asks, 'Why does today matter?'

A fulfilling retirement often needs both. Recreation restores. Contribution connects. Learning stretches.

Relationships give the experiences someone to share them with.

Do not turn every hobby into a mission statement. Do leave room for something beyond consumption.

Help Someone Else With Their List

The *Buried Life* concept included more than pursuing personal goals. The participants also helped other people accomplish dreams.

Imagine adding this retirement goal: Every year, help one person do something meaningful.

You might help a grandchild travel, fund a certification, mentor a new professional, support a family at church, teach a skill, assist an entrepreneur, make an introduction, or give someone the encouragement to try.

Your bucket list can collect experiences and create experiences for others. That is a powerful form of wealth.

You May Be Someone's Shortcut

What took you years to learn? Which errors could someone avoid? What question can you answer, door can you open, or standard can you model?

A retired contracting officer, scientist, manager, investigator, physician, technician, analyst, administrator, or tradesperson may possess knowledge younger professionals cannot download from a manual.

You do not need a prestigious title to have something valuable to teach. Patience, reliability, judgment, communication, parenthood, recovery, and ordinary life all create expertise.

Mentoring is a legacy with no probate process. One person helps another, who later helps someone else, and the influence keeps moving.

Know the Post-Government Rules

Retired federal employees may consult, work for contractors, serve organizations, or advocate on matters connected to their former agency. Certain post-government ethics restrictions can limit communications or appearances before the government on behalf of others, particularly concerning matters handled personally or under official responsibility.

Rules can differ by role, seniority, matter, timing, agency, and statute. Some restrictions are temporary; others can last much longer. Procurement, classified information, proprietary information, and professional licensing may add requirements.

Before accepting consulting or representation work, obtain guidance from the appropriate agency ethics office or qualified counsel. Do this before promising the client that your old colleagues will 'take the call.'

Experience is valuable. Use it without turning an act of contribution into a federal ethics refresher delivered by subpoena.

Maybe You Want to Keep Working

Some people genuinely enjoy work. Retirement does not require never earning another dollar.

You may consult, teach, work part-time, start a business, work seasonally, or redesign a career around the parts you loved while removing the commute, management, politics, and administrative tasks that consumed the joy.

Define the purpose: income, structure, connection, impact, challenge, or enjoyment. Decide how many hours of freedom you are willing to exchange.

There is a difference between working because retirement is unaffordable and choosing work because it remains meaningful. The financial plan is what makes the second sentence possible.

Federal Reemployment Has Special Rules

Returning to federal service can affect pay, annuity administration, retirement coverage, FEHB, FEGLI, and future benefits. Under the general reemployed-annuitant rule, federal salary may be reduced by the allocable annuity, although exceptions and dual-compensation waivers can apply.

The appointment type, retirement type, length of service, waiver authority, and benefit elections matter. Reemployment that suspends or terminates an annuity can create different consequences from ordinary salary-offset reemployment.

Obtain a written explanation from the hiring agency and verify the effect with OPM before accepting the position. Compare the gross salary, offset, taxes, benefits, schedule, and additional retirement credit—not merely the number in the job announcement.

A return to government should serve the purpose, not surprise the pension.

Give While You Can See the Impact

If the retirement plan shows resources beyond lifetime needs, survivor protection, and care reserves, some future inheritance may have greater impact today.

A child may be buying a home, a grandchild entering school, a church building something important, a charity meeting an urgent need, or a young person pursuing an opportunity you can help unlock.

Lifetime giving allows you to witness the result, share the story behind the gift, and teach the next generation. It can turn estate planning into living.

Financial independence comes first. Giving away money you may later need is not generosity to your future self or surviving spouse.

Generosity Needs Boundaries

Purpose-driven giving does not mean saying yes to every request. Decide whom and what the household wants to support, how much fits, and what conditions or limits matter.

Distinguish planned generosity from rescuing, guilt, pressure, and repeated financial dependency. Both spouses should understand significant gifts, particularly when they affect care reserves or survivor security.

Choose regular giving, occasional gifts, direct assistance, education, matching gifts, anonymous support, or legacy commitments according to the purpose.

A giving budget can sound less romantic than spontaneous generosity. It is often what allows generosity to continue.

Use the Tax Character of the Gift

Different assets can produce different charitable and family outcomes. Cash is simple. Appreciated securities may avoid realization of capital gain when given properly to a qualified charity. Pretax retirement money may be particularly efficient for charitable beneficiaries because qualified charities generally do not pay income tax.

A qualified charitable distribution generally must come directly from an IRA—not directly from the TSP—and is available only after the applicable statutory age and subject to current requirements and limits. A TSP-to-IRA rollover may create QCD flexibility but should be evaluated against costs, investment choices, creditor protection, and access rules.

Donor-advised funds, charitable trusts, life insurance, and beneficiary designations can serve different timing, control, tax, and family goals.

Start with the cause. Then ask tax and legal professionals to help more of the gift reach it.

Faith Can Occupy More of the Calendar

For many people, faith is central to purpose. During working years, worship, study, service, missions, generosity, mentoring, prayer, and community may have competed with the job and family schedule.

Retirement can create time to align the calendar more closely with a priority that was always important.

That does not mean every retiree must accept every committee position offered before the coffee is poured. Service should reflect gifts, season, health, and calling.

Purpose Driven Retirement asks whether time and resources match what you say matters. Faith is one of the clearest places to test the answer.

Time Is a Currency

Retirement may return thousands of hours each year. Those hours can be spent, wasted, invested, and given away just like money.

An hour helping with homework, an afternoon with a lonely friend, a morning mentoring, or three hours serving may produce a return no financial statement can measure.

Time also has limits. Protect health, marriage, rest, and personal goals. Generosity that creates resentment or exhaustion needs redesign.

Give time with the same intention used to give money: to people and purposes you actually value.

The Grandparent Dividend

Parents are often managing careers, school, sports, bills, and schedules. Grandparents may possess a resource the parents desperately need: time.

Time to listen, teach, attend, tell stories, share faith and family history, take a child fishing, practice a skill, or simply show up.

Grandchildren may never know the size of your TSP. They will remember whether they had access to you.

Be present without allowing the family to assume unlimited availability. The best contribution is intentional relationship, not permanent logistical duty.

Do Not Give Away Your Retirement

Generosity must remain coordinated with income, the spouse, healthcare, housing, taxes, emergencies, and long-term care.

Do not become financially dependent on children because you gave too much money to the children. Do not donate assets that were quietly assigned to the survivor's future.

Model gifts under reasonable and stressful scenarios. Use assets with attention to taxes and liquidity. Update the plan when health or markets change.

Boundaries do not weaken generosity. They protect the people and purposes the generosity is meant to serve.

Contribution Changes With Age

At sixty, contribution may involve boards, building projects, missions, consulting, travel, and active mentoring. At eighty, it may involve writing, calling, encouraging, giving, teaching grandchildren, sharing stories, or praying.

Purpose adapts to energy, health, caregiving, and season. It does not disappear because the method changes.

Being present can be a contribution. Listening can be service. A handwritten note can arrive at exactly the right moment.

Do not confuse a smaller radius of activity with a smaller life.

Avoid the Consumption Trap

Retirement advertising often follows a simple script: buy, travel, cruise, golf, eat, relax, repeat.

All of those can be wonderful. Enjoy the trip. Order dessert. Buy the boat if the plan supports it and someone genuinely wants to maintain a boat.

Thirty years of consumption alone can still become empty. People often need connection, growth, contribution, meaning, and somebody who benefits from their presence.

Purpose Driven Retirement does not reject enjoyment. It asks enjoyment to share the calendar with significance.

Ask the Eighty-Five-Year-Old You

Imagine being asked at eighty-five, 'What are you proudest of from retirement?'

Would you like to answer that you grew close to grandchildren, traveled with people you loved, helped younger professionals, served faithfully, gave more than expected, preserved family stories, supported a cause, or helped someone through a difficult season?

The answer does not need to be grand. It needs to sound like your values had somewhere to go.

That future answer can help choose today's calendar.

From Success to Significance

Working life often builds a career, reputation, home, savings, skill, and financial security. Retirement asks what you will do with what was built.

Some supports lifestyle. Some creates experiences. Some protects family. Some becomes inheritance. Some of your money, time, relationships, and knowledge may help another person build too.

That is where success can begin turning into significance.

Financial independence gives you the freedom to stop asking only what you have to do—and start deciding what is worth doing.

Your Purpose Driven Federal Employee Action Step

Create the Contribution Plan. Give time, expertise, and money assignments that fit the retirement rather than compete with it.

Experience Identify knowledge, judgment, skills, or relationships that could shorten someone else's learning curve.

People Name individuals, generations, communities, or causes you want to help.

Service Choose one sustainable volunteer, mentoring, faith, civic, or family contribution to test this year.

Work Define whether paid work serves income, structure, challenge, connection, or impact—and how much freedom it may use.

Federal rules Before consulting or reemployment, verify post-government ethics, salary offset, annuity, FEHB, FEGLI, and retirement consequences.

Complete the Giving and Significance Review

Giving capacity Determine what can be given without threatening lifetime income, the survivor, healthcare, housing, or care reserves.

Tax strategy Coordinate cash, appreciated assets, IRAs, TSP, insurance, charitable vehicles, and beneficiary designations with qualified professionals.

Family Decide how children and grandchildren will participate in service, giving, stories, education, and shared values.

One dream Choose one person whose bucket-list goal you can help advance.

Future answer Write what you hope to be proudest of at age eighty-five—and put the first action on the calendar.

Your federal title may end, but the experience and capacity accumulated behind it remain. Retirement gives you the freedom to decide where they go next. Use some of that freedom for yourself, and some to make another person's life better.

Chapter 16

Your Purpose Driven Federal Retirement Plan

We have covered a great deal together: eligibility, service history, pension calculations, the FERS supplement, Social Security, TSP, FEHB, PSHB, Medicare, taxes, insurance, survivor protection, long-term care, estate planning, relationships, health, giving, and purpose.

At times, the federal rules may have felt complicated. They are. Uncle Sam has never been accused of using one page when a handbook and three forms were available.

Yet retirement planning begins with one simple question: What matters most to you?

Everything else—every calculation, election, account, and form—is the work of helping those things become more likely to happen.

The Plan Is Not the Purpose

The financial plan is not the goal. The TSP balance is not the goal. The pension, Social Security strategy, tax conversion, Medicare choice, and insurance contract are not the goal.

They are tools. The goal may be time with a spouse, travel, grandchildren, independence, service, faith, generosity, family protection, another business, a meaningful legacy, or waking up knowing the day belongs to you.

A technically perfect benefit election that does not support the life you want is an impressive answer to the wrong question.

The plan exists to serve the purpose. Never permit the tools to become more important than the people using them.

Begin With 'What Matters Most?'

If you remember only one question from this book, remember this one.

Do not begin with what the market did, the best TSP fund, the perfect Social Security age, the current tax bracket, or the retirement number your coworker announced after lunch.

Begin by identifying what the resources must protect and create. Without that answer, accumulation has no assignment and optimization has no standard.

The life comes first. Then the math.

This Book Is a Guide, Not a One-Time Read

A Purpose Driven Federal Retirement is meant to remain useful after the first reading. Return to it before retirement, during the OPM application process, after the first annuity statement, when Medicare begins, before Social Security or RMDs, after a death or diagnosis, and whenever the life vision changes.

Write in it. Use the checklists. Update the bucket list. Recalculate the survivor plan. Revisit the tax window. Confirm beneficiaries. Bring questions to professional meetings.

Rules change, but the planning sequence remains valuable: define the purpose, understand the benefit, test the interactions, make the decision, implement it, and review the result.

This is not a book to finish and admire. It is a guide to use.

Build the Plan With Five Questions

The entire framework can be organized around five questions.

What matters most? What should retirement look like? What must the money and federal benefits accomplish? What could knock the plan off course? What needs to happen now?

These questions move from life to strategy to risk to action. They prevent the household from selecting products and elections before deciding what problem needs to be solved.

Take out a page and title it: My Purpose Driven Federal Retirement Plan.

1. What Matters Most?

Write the five things that matter most. Not twenty. Five.

They may include a spouse, family, faith, health, independence, service, adventure, security, community, or legacy. Your answers should be personal; federal retirement law does not prescribe them.

Then rank them when priorities compete. More travel can reduce legacy. More survivor protection can reduce current pension income. A later retirement can improve benefits while postponing healthy years.

A priority becomes useful when it helps choose between two good options.

2. What Should Retirement Look Like?

Describe an ordinary week and the important years. Where will you live? Who will be nearby? What will you do Monday? How will health, relationships, service, learning, rest, faith, and fun appear?

List the large and everyday bucket-list goals. Identify which belong in the active, steady, and support years. Name the people who should share them.

Discuss the vision separately and together with a spouse. Do not assume two people interpret 'travel more' or 'help the kids' the same way.

Make retirement tangible enough that the financial plan can recognize it.

3. What Must the Money and Benefits Accomplish?

Now bring in the pension, Social Security, TSP, other assets, FEHB or PSHB, Medicare, insurance, housing, and taxes.

How much after-tax income is needed? Which expenses are essential? What bridges the gap before Social Security? What job belongs to traditional and Roth TSP money? How much liquidity protects against delayed OPM processing and unexpected costs?

Which survivor election preserves income and healthcare? How will long-term care be funded? Which assets should be spent, converted, insured, given, or left to beneficiaries?

Every benefit needs an assignment connected to the life. A benefit without a job tends to receive one accidentally from taxes, markets, or an emergency.

4. What Could Knock the Plan Off Course?

Test the plan against market declines, inflation, early death, long life, care needs, tax changes, a delayed pension, higher spending, relocation, health changes, family requests, and an earlier-than-planned separation.

Federal benefits reduce some risks without removing them. A pension supplies income but may lose purchasing power. FEHB provides medical coverage but not unlimited custodial care. TSP creates flexibility but also investment and tax decisions.

The goal is not to predict every event. It is to build reserves, protections, and decision rules that allow the plan to adapt when reality declines to follow the spreadsheet.

Flexibility is a retirement asset too.

5. What Must Happen Now?

This may be the most important question. What action needs to happen now—not someday?

Verify service, update beneficiaries, choose the retirement date, increase savings, change investments, build cash, model Roth conversions, review insurance, complete estate documents, schedule healthcare, discuss the survivor election, create the bucket list, or have the family meeting.

Write the owner and date beside every action. 'We should' is not an owner. 'Soon' is not a date.

A plan without implementation is information wearing business-casual clothing.

The Doctor's Office

Return to the story from the introduction. Imagine visiting the doctor for a physical while excitedly discussing a child's wedding and the possibility of becoming a grandparent.

The results arrive. Blood pressure is dangerously high. Cholesterol is severely elevated. The doctor explains that without changes and appropriate treatment, you may not be around to enjoy the people and events you just said matter most.

Imagine responding, 'Thank you for letting me know. Let me think about it,' and then doing nothing.

If being present for the family truly matters, the recommendation is not merely about numbers on a laboratory report. It is connected to a life you want. Financial planning works the same way.

'Let Me Think About It'

Thoughtful consideration is appropriate. Major decisions deserve questions, understanding, comparison, and sometimes a second opinion. Never implement a recommendation you do not understand.

There is also a difference between consideration and indefinite procrastination. Sometimes 'let me think about it' means change is uncomfortable, the decision is difficult, or later feels easier.

Meanwhile, the beneficiary remains outdated, the tax window closes, the survivor election approaches, insurance becomes unavailable, the portfolio remains mismatched, and the bucket-list trip loses another healthy year.

Eventually, time makes the decision. It rarely asks whether the result matched your intentions.

If It Matters, Act Like It Matters

If the spouse's financial security matters, protect it. If travel matters, schedule it. If grandchildren matter, give them time. If legacy matters, define it. If health matters, act on it. If faith and service matter, place them on the calendar.

If avoiding unnecessary taxes matters, use the legal planning opportunities Judge Learned Hand reminded taxpayers they are permitted to use. If the retirement vision matters, complete the decisions required to fund it.

Knowing the rule does not update a designation, submit an application, convert an account, purchase protection, or book a trip.

Purpose without action is intention. Implementation is what gives purpose a chance to become life.

You Do Not Need a Perfect Plan

Some people wait for certainty about markets, inflation, taxes, longevity, healthcare costs, politics, or the exact year a roof will decide it has served long enough.

Those answers are unavailable. A good retirement plan is not a prediction. It is a framework for making reasonable decisions amid uncertainty.

Use current law and conservative assumptions. Build margins. Maintain liquidity. Protect catastrophic risks. Review regularly. Change course when the evidence changes.

You do not need perfection. You need direction and the willingness to move.

The Federal Retirement Launch Plan

In the final working year, assemble the service record, estimates, survivor analysis, FEHB or PSHB history, FEGLI elections, TSP strategy, tax plan, leave projections, and application timeline. Resolve discrepancies before the final week.

Before separation, retain personal copies of relevant records and contact information. Confirm beneficiaries and insurance. Build cash for the interim-pay period. Coordinate payroll deductions, allotments, and the first months without a normal paycheck.

After retirement, review interim payments, the final OPM adjudication, the annuity statement, tax withholding, survivor reduction, insurance deductions, health premiums, leave payment, TSP access, and Social Security timing. Correct errors promptly.

Retirement is not complete when the farewell email is sent. The launch continues until the benefits arrive as intended.

Use a Specialist Who Understands the System

Federal planning is specialized because one choice can affect several benefits. The retirement date can affect pension, supplement, COLA timing, leave, FEHB, TSP access, and taxes. The survivor election can affect income and healthcare. A TSP withdrawal can affect tax brackets and IRMAA.

A professional with the Chartered Federal Employee Benefits Consultant℠ (ChFEBC℠) designation has specialized training in federal benefits. That does not replace legal, tax, insurance, or medical professionals, and no designation removes the obligation to verify current rules.

It does help identify a planner who understands that 'the pension' is not one number and 'keep FEHB' is not the entire retirement strategy.

The value is coordination and implementation—not merely another explanation of the acronyms.

Review Purpose Before Performance

At the annual review, do not begin with investment performance. Begin with: What matters most now?

Are time and money being used that way? Is the survivor still protected? Has health changed? Is a goal being postponed? Do benefits, taxes, insurance, beneficiaries, housing, and care plans still support the life?

Then review performance, allocation, withdrawals, conversions, RMDs, tax withholding, Medicare, OPM records, and cash needs.

That order keeps the portfolio accountable to the purpose instead of allowing the statement to define success.

Your Number Is Not the Answer

One million dollars is not a retirement plan. Neither is two million or ten million.

The useful number is the amount and structure of resources required to support the life, risks, taxes, people, and flexibility that matter to the household.

A federal pension and continued health coverage can reduce the portfolio needed for essential income. A large legacy goal, early retirement, extensive travel, care risk, or survivor need can increase it.

The number follows the life. It cannot define the life by itself.

The Real Return on the Money

Investment statements measure percentages. Retirement introduces another return: what did the money create?

Did it buy freedom, protect a spouse, preserve independence, create memories, educate grandchildren, support faith, help another person, fund care, and give the household time?

Those returns will never appear beside the C Fund, G Fund, or an advisory account. They may be the most important returns the assets produce.

A successful plan should still care about prudent performance. It should remember why performance mattered.

You Do Not Have to Do This Alone

You may finish this book thinking two things: This is important—and this is a lot.

You do not need to become an expert in retirement law, TSP, Social Security, Medicare, taxes, insurance, estate planning, and every federal form. You do need to identify the decisions, ask good questions, and make sure somebody is coordinating them.

If you would like help organizing the pieces or obtaining a second opinion, Purpose Driven Retirement Planners offers a no-cost, no-obligation conversation. Bring the plan you have, the one you have not started, or the one question keeping you awake.

Good planning should not begin with a product. It should begin with understanding what matters most to you. Schedule at www.calendly.com/pdrp or use the book's scheduling QR code.

Your Final Assignment

Before closing this chapter, write the three things that matter most.

Then write one action you will complete within thirty days to move life closer to those priorities. Not ten actions. One completed action.

Tell the person affected. Put it on the calendar. Gather the document. Make the appointment. Submit the form. Begin.

The purpose of this book was never only to teach federal retirement. It was to help you do something with what you learned.

Your Purpose Driven Federal Employee Action Step

Complete the one-page plan. Use it now, during the retirement transition, and throughout life as benefits, health, family, and purpose change.

Five priorities Write the five things that matter most and rank them when they compete.

Retirement vision Describe the ordinary week, retirement seasons, home, people, bucket list, health, service, and legacy.

Benefit assignments Give the pension, supplement, Social Security, TSP, FEHB or PSHB, Medicare, insurance, and other assets specific jobs.

Risk response Document reserves and actions for markets, inflation, long life, early death, care, taxes, health, and delayed benefits.

Turn the Plan Into Action

Launch checklist Verify service, forms, beneficiaries, survivor elections, coverage, cash, taxes, leave, and the OPM adjudication.

Annual review Review purpose first, then benefits, investments, taxes, beneficiaries, insurance, housing, care, and action items.

Professional team Identify the ChFEBC-trained planner, tax professional, estate attorney, insurance specialists, and other advisers responsible for coordination.

Thirty-day action Choose one decision or task, name the owner, set the deadline, and complete it.

Do not just retire. Build a retirement around what matters most, use the federal benefits for the jobs they were meant to do, and take the actions that give the life you have planned a genuine chance to happen. That is A Purpose Driven Federal Retirement.

Conclusion

Don't Just Retire. Retire With Purpose.

Someday, your federal career will end. The last payroll deposit will arrive. Your badge, credential, laptop, keys, or parking pass will be returned. The calendar that belonged partly to an agency will begin belonging more fully to you.

All the years spent serving, saving, contributing to the TSP, earning the pension, accumulating leave, protecting FEHB, and postponing parts of life will have purchased something extraordinarily valuable: time.

What will you do with it?

That is the question behind this entire book. Not whether you selected the mathematically perfect fund on every date. Not whether you claimed every benefit at the single theoretical moment a spreadsheet preferred. Those decisions matter only because they support something larger.

Your life. Your spouse. Your family. Your health. Your independence. Your experiences. Your generosity. Your legacy. Your purpose.

The Benefits Were Never the Destination

FERS or CSRS, Social Security, TSP, FEHB or PSHB, Medicare, FEGLI, and the other benefits in this book are powerful tools. They are not the retirement itself.

The pension can protect essential income. Social Security can protect longevity and a surviving spouse. TSP can fund flexibility, goals, care, and legacy. Health coverage can protect access and the balance sheet. Tax planning can preserve more of every resource for the work you intended it to do.

A toolbox can be exceptionally well organized and still build nothing. The value appears when the tools are used for a life.

Do Not Protect Every Dollar From Its Purpose

Some retirees become so focused on preserving assets that they never give the money permission to perform the job for which it was accumulated.

Do not spend recklessly. Protect income, the survivor, healthcare, long-term care, housing, taxes, and emergencies. Prepare for what can go wrong.

Then give yourself permission to live. Take the trip. Create the family memory. Learn the skill. Help someone. Make the gift. Improve the home. Use time with the people who matter while the window is open.

The highest possible ending balance is not automatically evidence of the best possible retirement.

Keep Asking the Purpose Question

Before every major retirement decision, ask: Does this move us closer to what matters most?

Does working another year create security we genuinely need, or postpone a healthy year we cannot replace? Does the withdrawal fund a meaningful goal, or merely satisfy an impulse? Does the survivor election protect the person we said mattered? Does the tax strategy improve lifetime flexibility? Does the home support the life and care plan?

The purpose question does not make every answer easy. It makes the tradeoff visible.

When the plan becomes confusing, return to that question. It is the compass for the entire guide.

The Doctor's Warning Only Helps If You Act

Remember the doctor who explains that dangerous blood pressure and cholesterol may prevent a patient from enjoying the wedding, grandchild, and future they just described.

The diagnosis creates knowledge. The prescription creates a possible path. Neither improves the outcome if the patient thanks the doctor, says 'I'll think about it,' and changes nothing.

This book has identified retirement versions of the same moment: an incorrect service record, an unprotected spouse, an oversized pretax account, an approaching tax window, outdated beneficiaries, missing insurance, no long-term-care plan, and important goals postponed without a date.

Information is the beginning of planning. Action is what gives the information value.

Use the Guide Throughout Life

Return to this book when retirement approaches, benefits begin, Medicare starts, Social Security is claimed, RMDs draw near, health changes, a spouse dies, the family grows, or the purpose evolves.

Revisit the retirement vision before the portfolio. Update the bucket list. Confirm the benefit records. Recalculate taxes and survivor income. Review care, beneficiaries, insurance, housing, and the people authorized to help.

The book is not a test you pass once. It is a guide for decisions that unfold across decades.

Federal rules will change. Your life will change. The habit of connecting every resource to what matters most should remain.

The Measure That Matters

Eventually, the most important measure of retirement will not be the amount left in every account.

It will be whether the resources helped you live the life you said mattered: whether they created freedom, protected people, preserved dignity, supported health, opened opportunities, funded generosity, and gave purpose room to become action.

A successful federal retirement is not merely one in which OPM calculated the annuity correctly—although we would certainly prefer that too.

It is one in which the benefits earned through a career of service became the foundation for a life lived intentionally afterward.

Your Closing Promise

Complete these sentences before you move to the final invitation.

The three things that matter most to me are:

____

The federal benefit decision that most needs attention is:

____

The experience or relationship I should stop postponing is:

____

One action I will complete within thirty days is:

____

Tell someone. Set the date. Make the call. Submit the form. Schedule the meeting. Begin.

Do not just retire. Retire with purpose—and act like the purpose matters.

You Don't Have to Do This Alone

If you have made it this far, you may be thinking two things at the same time:

"This is important."

and

"This is a lot."

That is understandable. Federal retirement can involve eligibility, service records, pensions, survivor elections, TSP, Social Security, FEHB or PSHB, Medicare, taxes, insurance, long-term care, estate planning, beneficiaries, family—and the larger question of what all those resources are supposed to accomplish.

You do not need to become an expert in every area. You do not need to arrive with everything organized. Sometimes the most valuable next step is simply sitting down with someone who understands the federal system and can help identify what deserves attention first.

The team at Purpose Driven Retirement Planners would be happy to meet with you for a no-cost, no-obligation conversation. Bring your questions, concerns, goals, benefit estimates, or the retirement plan you have not started yet.

The conversation begins with understanding—not a product—and with the same question that began this book: What matters most to you?

Schedule a Conversation

Maybe you need a complete federal retirement plan.

Maybe you need a second opinion or one question answered.

Maybe you simply need help deciding where to begin.

Either way, you do not have to navigate the next chapter alone.

SCAN TO SCHEDULE

www.calendly.com/pdrp

No cost. No obligation.

Just a conversation about what matters most to you.

PURPOSE DRIVEN
RETIREMENT PLANNERS

PDRPlanners.com | 804-499-3144

Helping you build a retirement around what matters most—and use it for what matters next.

Selected References

Where to Verify the Rules Before You Act

Federal retirement planning is full of rules, exceptions, effective dates, forms, and acronyms that occasionally appear to be breeding when no one is watching. The sources below provide a practical starting point for checking the current rules behind this book.

Use the current online version of every source. Agency pages, forms, thresholds, carrier arrangements, and procedures can change after publication. When a decision affects retirement eligibility, survivor protection, health coverage, taxes, or an irrevocable election, confirm it with the responsible agency and the appropriate qualified professional before acting.

This is a selected reading list, not a citation for every sentence. It favors primary government and program sources so readers can verify changing rules without first wandering through six sponsored articles and a pop-up asking whether they are ready to retire by Thursday.

Federal Retirement, Insurance, and Health Benefits

OPM Retirement Center. https://www.opm.gov/retirement-center/ — Retirement systems, planning, applications, survivor benefits, and retiree services.

OPM CSRS/FERS Handbook. https://www.opm.gov/retirement-center/publications-forms/csrsfers-handbook/ — Detailed federal retirement guidance; check later laws and current OPM guidance because portions of the handbook are older.

OPM Retirement Publications and Forms. https://www.opm.gov/retirement-center/publications-forms/ — Current pamphlets, forms, and Benefits Administration Letters.

OPM FERS Information. https://www.opm.gov/retirement-center/fers-information/ — Eligibility, computation, service credit, survivor benefits, and application guidance.

OPM CSRS Information. https://www.opm.gov/retirement-center/csrs-information/ — CSRS and CSRS Offset topics.

OPM FEHB Handbook. https://www.opm.gov/healthcare-insurance/healthcare/reference-materials/fehb-handbook/ — Enrollment, family-member eligibility, continuation into retirement, and program administration.

OPM Postal Service Health Benefits Program. https://www.opm.gov/healthcare-insurance/pshb/ — Current PSHB information for Postal Service employees, annuitants, and eligible family members.

OPM Federal Employees' Group Life Insurance. https://www.opm.gov/healthcare-insurance/life-insurance/ — FEGLI coverage, elections, forms, and retirement information.

Federal Long Term Care Insurance Program. https://www.ltcfeds.com/ — Official program information, including current enrollment status and coverage administration.

Thrift Savings Plan

TSP Official Website. https://www.tsp.gov/ — Account access, current plan rules, tools, forms, and notices.

TSP Publications. https://www.tsp.gov/publications/ — Current booklets and fact sheets covering distributions, taxes, death benefits, loans, and other plan topics.

TSP Withdrawals in Retirement. https://www.tsp.gov/withdrawals-in-retirement/ — Installments, partial and total distributions, required distributions, and life-annuity information.

TSP Required Minimum Distributions. https://www.tsp.gov/withdrawals-in-retirement/required-minimum-distributions/ — Current TSP RMD procedures and timing.

TSP Beneficiary Designations. https://www.tsp.gov/tsp-basics/designating-beneficiaries/ — How beneficiary designations work and how to review them.

For any TSP life annuity decision, obtain and read the current TSP annuity materials and the insurer's current terms. The TSP life annuity is purchased through the TSP's private-insurer arrangement; it requires annuitization, exchanges account value for a contractual income stream, and can be difficult or impossible to reverse. Verify the current carrier, options, rates, survivor features, and refund provisions before signing anything.

Social Security and Medicare

Social Security Retirement Benefits. https://www.ssa.gov/retirement — Claiming, estimates, eligibility, and current retirement-benefit guidance.

Social Security Survivor Benefits. https://www.ssa.gov/survivor — Eligibility and application guidance for survivors.

Social Security Medicare Information. https://www.ssa.gov/medicare — Enrollment and premium-related information.

Request to Lower an IRMAA. https://www.ssa.gov/medicare/lower-irmaa — Current SSA guidance and Form SSA-44 process after certain life-changing events.

Medicare & You. https://www.medicare.gov/medicare-and-you — The current official Medicare handbook.

Medicare Costs. https://www.medicare.gov/basics/costs/medicare-costs — Current premiums, deductibles, and cost-sharing information.

Medicare Long-Term-Care Coverage. https://www.medicare.gov/coverage/long-term-care — What Medicare generally does and does not cover.

Social Security law has changed before and will change again. Confirm current treatment of CSRS, CSRS Offset, FERS, spousal and survivor benefits, and any prior noncovered employment directly with SSA before relying on an estimate.

Federal Tax Guidance

IRS Publication 721. https://www.irs.gov/publications/p721 — Tax Guide to U.S. Civil Service Retirement Benefits.

IRS Publication 590-A. https://www.irs.gov/publications/p590a — Contributions to Individual Retirement Arrangements.

IRS Publication 590-B. https://www.irs.gov/publications/p590b — IRA distributions, including required distributions and beneficiary rules.

IRS Publication 915. https://www.irs.gov/publications/p915 — Taxation of Social Security benefits.

IRS Publication 969. https://www.irs.gov/publications/p969 — Health savings accounts and other tax-favored health plans.

IRS Retirement Plans and IRA Required Minimum Distributions FAQs. https://www.irs.gov/retirement-plans/retirement-plan-and-ira-required-minimum-distributions-faqs — Current federal RMD guidance.

Ethics, Investing, and Professional Guidance

U.S. Office of Government Ethics—Post-Government Employment. https://www.oge.gov/web/oge.nsf/Resources/OGE+Issues+Plain+Language+Discussion+for+Agency+Ethics+Officials,+Departing+Employees,+and+Former+Employees+on+the+Post-Government+Employment+Restrictions — Plain-language discussion of restrictions that may apply after federal service.

SEC Investor.gov. https://www.investor.gov/ — Independent investor education, risk, fees, fraud prevention, and professional-background tools.

Employees subject to agency-specific ethics rules, financial-disclosure requirements, security restrictions, or post-employment limits should consult their agency ethics office before separation and before accepting outside work.

Important Disclosures

Please Read This Before Making Decisions With Real Consequences

Educational Purpose

This book is for general educational and informational purposes. It is not individualized financial, investment, tax, legal, accounting, insurance, benefits, estate-planning, or medical advice, and it is not a recommendation to buy, sell, retain, roll over, surrender, exchange, or annuitize any investment or insurance product. Examples are simplified to teach concepts and may omit facts that would materially change an actual recommendation.

Rules Change—and Your Facts Matter

The discussion reflects the author's understanding of laws, rules, program features, and publicly available guidance as of August 2026. Congress, agencies, courts, tax authorities, plan administrators, insurers, and carriers may change laws, interpretations, thresholds, forms, procedures, products, and contractual terms at any time. Dollar limits and tax thresholds commonly change from year to year.

Your benefit is governed by applicable law, official records, plan documents, agency determinations, and contracts—not by this book, an online calculator, or a friendly estimate written on the back of a lunch receipt. Verify service history, eligibility, elections, deadlines, beneficiary records, and benefit estimates with your agency, OPM, the TSP, SSA, Medicare, the IRS, and any other responsible administrator.

Professional Advice

Consult appropriately licensed or credentialed professionals who can evaluate your complete circumstances. Tax decisions should be reviewed with a qualified tax professional; legal and estate documents with an attorney admitted in the relevant jurisdiction; benefits elections with the responsible agency or administrator; insurance with a properly licensed professional; and health or care decisions with qualified medical and care professionals.

A professional designation describes education or training under the issuing organization's standards. It does not guarantee competence, results, regulatory approval, or a particular outcome. Confirm a professional's current credentials, licenses, registrations, disciplinary history, services, compensation, and conflicts before engaging them.

ChFEBC and Government Non-Endorsement

The Chartered Federal Employee Benefits Consultant℠ (ChFEBC℠) designation identifies specialized training concerning federal employee benefits. It can help a planner understand how federal benefits interact, but it does not replace official agency guidance, individual analysis, or the advice of tax and legal professionals.

The author and Purpose Driven Retirement Planners are not affiliated with, employed by, sponsored by, or endorsed by the United States government, OPM, the Federal Retirement Thrift Investment Board, the Thrift Savings Plan, SSA, CMS, Medicare, the IRS, OGE, or any federal agency. Use of agency and program names is descriptive. The ChFEBC designation is not a federal-government credential or endorsement.

Investments, Rollovers, and Taxes

All investing involves risk, including possible loss of principal. Past performance does not predict future results. No allocation, withdrawal method, conversion schedule, or tax strategy can guarantee income, returns, tax savings, Medicare-premium results, or protection from loss. Projections depend on assumptions that may prove wrong.

A rollover or transfer may affect investment choices, expenses, services, withdrawal rights, creditor protection, beneficiary treatment, required distributions, and access to plan-specific features. Moving money from the TSP is not automatically better—or worse—than leaving it there. Compare the actual alternatives and disclose all costs and conflicts before acting.

Tax planning involves current and future rates, filing status, deductions, credits, state law, Social Security taxation, RMDs, IRMAA, charitable goals, estate rules, and beneficiary circumstances. A strategy that lowers this year's tax bill can increase another year's cost. Coordinate before executing Roth conversions, large withdrawals, gifts, beneficiary changes, or account transfers.

Insurance and Annuities

Annuities are contracts, not a single product category. Features vary widely. Some modern annuities may provide contractual income benefits without irrevocably annuitizing the account; others, including a TSP life annuity election, require annuitization. Annuitization generally means exchanging control of principal for the insurer's contractual promise of payments under the option selected. The election may be irrevocable, and liquidity, inflation protection, survivor income, and any remaining value depend on the contract.

Annuity and insurance guarantees depend on the issuing insurer's claims-paying ability and applicable contract terms. Products may include fees, caps, spreads, participation limits, surrender charges, market-value adjustments, exclusions, tax consequences, and restrictions. Review the carrier, contract, state approval, costs, liquidity, death benefit, income method, and alternatives. No statement in this book means that all annuities are good, all annuities are bad, or that one contract fits everyone.

Long-Term Care, Estate Planning, and Beneficiaries

Long-term-care needs, costs, eligibility, insurance availability, and family capacity are uncertain. Medicare is not comprehensive long-term-care insurance. Medicaid eligibility and estate-recovery rules vary and require current, state-specific advice. Any care-funding illustration is educational only.

Beneficiary designations, survivor elections, wills, trusts, powers of attorney, and account titles can interact in unexpected ways. Do not assume a will controls every account. Review these items together with qualified counsel and each account or benefit administrator, especially after marriage, divorce, death, birth, disability, or a move to another state.

Final Responsibility

The reader remains responsible for decisions and for confirming current information. Neither the author nor the publisher promises that every source will remain available or that every web address will remain unchanged. Product names and trademarks belong to their respective owners.

The point of these disclosures is not to frighten you into doing nothing. Doing nothing is still a decision—and sometimes an expensive one. Use this book to ask better questions, verify the answers, and take informed action while your choices are still choices.

About the Author

Stuart Hunsicker

Founder, Purpose Driven Retirement Planners

Stuart Hunsicker has spent more than two decades helping individuals and families navigate some of the most important financial decisions of their lives. His dedication to financial planning, however, began with something far more personal than numbers.

Personal loss gave Stuart an early understanding of the financial consequences an unexpected life event can leave behind for the people we love. That experience helped shape a philosophy that has guided his career ever since: financial planning is not simply about accumulating more money. It is about using the resources we have to protect the people we care about and create the life we want to live.

Today, Stuart brings that philosophy to his work with retirees, pre-retirees, federal employees, educators, families, and business owners. His approach emphasizes comprehensive planning—coordinating retirement income, Social Security, pensions, investments, taxes, healthcare, long-term care, estate planning, risk management, and legacy rather than treating each decision in isolation.

That philosophy became the foundation for Purpose Driven Retirement and, now, A Purpose Driven Federal Retirement.

What Matters Most?

Stuart believes a successful retirement begins with a question much bigger than "How much money do I need?" It begins with: What matters most?

Once that answer is clear, the financial decisions have a purpose. Social Security is not simply a government benefit. Investments are not simply account balances. A pension is not simply a monthly check. Taxes are not simply something to minimize. They are tools that can be coordinated to help create financial independence, protect a spouse, care for family, pursue meaningful experiences, give generously, and live retirement with intention.

A Special Focus on Federal Employees

Federal employees occupy a distinctive planning world. A retirement decision can affect the FERS or CSRS annuity, survivor protection, the FERS supplement, TSP access, FEHB or PSHB, FEGLI, Social Security, Medicare, taxes, and the benefits available to a surviving spouse—sometimes all at once.

Stuart's work with federal employees is supported by specialized training through the Chartered Federal Employee Benefits Consultant℠ (ChFEBC℠) and Federal Retirement Consultant℠ (FRC℠) designations. The ChFEBC curriculum focuses on the federal benefit system and the planning decisions surrounding it. That training helps a financial professional understand how the pieces interact—not merely how each acronym is spelled, although federal employment provides plenty of practice with that too.

A designation does not replace OPM, the TSP, SSA, Medicare, the IRS, an agency benefits office, or qualified legal and tax advice. It does, however, help a planner ask better questions, recognize federal-specific consequences, and coordinate benefits with the rest of a household's financial life.

Experience, Education, and Life Beyond the Office

Now in his 21st year in financial services, Stuart has pursued extensive advanced education across multiple areas of financial and retirement planning. He earned his bachelor's degree in Business with a concentration in Finance from Virginia Commonwealth University in 2005 and is currently enrolled in a master's program in Business Leadership.

Stuart lives in Richmond, Virginia, with his wife, Andrea, their two children, and a bevy of cats. Away from financial planning, he is an avid sports fan who enjoys concerts, travel, and spending as much of his free time as possible with family. The cats remain enthusiastic supporters of retirement planning, provided the plan preserves adequate resources for food and ownership of every available chair.

He is the Founder of Purpose Driven Retirement Planners, whose mission reflects the philosophy behind this book: To provide transformational guidance helping people's retirement dreams become reality.

Core Professional Designations

Specialized knowledge supporting comprehensive retirement planning

ChFEBC℠ — Chartered Federal Employee Benefits Consultant℠. Specialized education concerning federal retirement and employee benefits.

FRC℠ — Federal Retirement Consultant℠. Training focused on federal retirement decisions and benefit coordination.

ChFC® — Chartered Financial Consultant®. Comprehensive financial-planning education spanning investments, insurance, tax, retirement, and estate considerations.

RICP® — Retirement Income Certified Professional®. Advanced education focused on converting retirement resources into sustainable income.

NSSA® — National Social Security Advisor®. Specialized education concerning Social Security claiming and household coordination.

TPCP™ — Tax Planning Certified Professional™. Training in proactive tax-planning concepts and their connection to broader financial decisions.

Certified Financial Fiduciary® — Certified Financial Fiduciary®. Education concerning fiduciary principles and putting a client's interests first.

CERTCFC® — Certified Christian Financial Counselor®. Training that integrates financial counseling with faith, stewardship, and purpose.

Why These Credentials Appear Here

Credentials are not trophies for a bookshelf. Their value is the perspective they bring to the people being served.

Federal retirement rarely fits inside a single specialty. Pension elections affect survivors. TSP withdrawals affect taxes. Taxes may affect Medicare premiums. Healthcare choices affect cash flow. Long-term-care risks affect the spouse, estate, and legacy. A strong plan requires enough breadth to see the household—and enough federal specialization to understand the rules that make the household unusual.

No credential guarantees advice, results, or government endorsement. Readers should evaluate the professional, the planning process, services, compensation, licenses, registrations, experience, and conflicts—not merely the letters after a name.

Professional Education & Credentials

- Certified Financial Education Instructor℠ / CFEI®
- ChFEBC℠ — Chartered Federal Employee Benefits Consultant℠
- ChFC® — Chartered Financial Consultant®
- CEPA® — Certified Exit Planning Advisor®
- CVGA® — Certified Value Growth Advisor®
- CLU® — Chartered Life Underwriter®
- CLTC® — Certification in Long Term Care
- CRPS® — Chartered Retirement Plans Specialist℠
- ABFP® — Accredited Behavioral Finance Professional℠
- AWMA® — Accredited Wealth Management Advisor℠
- ASBC® — Accredited Small Business Consultant®
- TPCP™ — Tax Planning Certified Professional™
- RICP® — Retirement Income Certified Professional®
- CRPC® — Chartered Retirement Planning Counselor℠
- CMFA® — Certified Military Financial Advisor
- CERTCFC® — Certified Christian Financial Counselor®
- Certified Financial Fiduciary®
- IRMAACP® — IRMAA Certified Planner®
- NSSA® — National Social Security Advisor®
- MFP — Master Financial Planner®
- FRC℠ — Federal Retirement Consultant℠

PURPOSE DRIVEN
RETIREMENT PLANNERS

Purpose Driven Retirement Planners

PDRPlanners.com | 804-499-3144

Helping you build a retirement around what matters most—and use it for what matters next.

www.ingramcontent.com/pod-product-compliance
Lightning Source LLC
LaVergne TN
LVHW100139061126
851857LV00010B/149
* 9 7 9 8 9 9 7 7 4 5 2 7 1 *